FRESH FROM THE KITCHEN

FRESH AND CREATIVE KNOWLEDGE ON LIFE AND LEADERSHIP

2ND EDITION - 2015

FRANK KITCHEN

Kyra,

Thank you for your patience. I'll be following you and the women's soccer team. I hope my words inspire you!

Live FRESH!

MOtivational PRESS
LEADERS IN GLOBAL PUBLISHING

Published by Motivational Press, Inc.
7777 N Wickham Rd, # 12-247
Melbourne, FL 32940
www.MotivationalPress.com

Manufactured in the United States of America.

ISBN: 978-1-62865-167-6

CONTENTS

FORWARD

BY RODGER N. CAMPBELL

Like a bolt of lightning in the evening sky, inspiration strikes with power, brightens the world, and powerfully energizes everything in its path. It can surge while you quietly watch an evening sunset at the beach. It can pulse during the drive home from work while listening to your favorite song. It can explode while you're at home with friends, enjoying a meal fresh from the kitchen. Inspiration strikes when you least expect it, but just when it is needed. You picked up this book because the time is right for inspiration.

Wherever he is, Frank Kitchen is that inspirational bolt of lighting. He brightens the world with his passion to serve, and powerfully energizes with his wit and encouragement. For over a decade, I've experienced Frank's wit and candor. His quiet demeanor masks his sharp insight, which he shares in his unique story-telling style. His life has been a winding journey full of ups and downs, twist and turns, giving him well-seasoned stories rich with the full flavor of real life. Watching him pursue his dream with a steady resolve has inspired and challenged me just to keep up.

In this book you too will be exposed to Frank's humor, insight, but most of all his heart. Helping individuals believe in themselves and their dreams is his passion. He possesses the uncanny ability to put light on an obvious subject, which transcends the surface and gets to the core of the matter. He's often said: "I might not be the smartest person in the world, but I have eyes." I think he's just being humble. Without a doubt, Frank has big eyes with extremely keen vision. He will challenge you to look beyond what you think you see to view what is really there:

possibilities. His fresh ideas are hot, like a good meal, and just as filling. Your stomach will be full of laughter and your heart warmed, the sign of a great meal. Grab a comfy chair, get your cozy blanket, sit back and enjoy the "culinary" delights Frank has whipped up for you. Some stories might be a bit "hot," but you'll always know it is Fresh from the Kitchen.

ACKNOWLEDGMENTS

Dear Family, Friends, and Readers,

I would like to thank you for investing in my book. Without your support, this book would not be possible. Life is about relationships and experiences. The relationships I have cultivated have allowed me to share my experiences with you in this book.

There were a lot of people who played roles in the writing of "Fresh from the Kitchen."

My wife Kelly is the amazing woman that I am forever indebted to. Her physical, fiscal, and emotional support gave me the motivation I needed to pursue this experience. I am truly blessed to have her in my life. Thank you, *AGP,* for sharing your life with me.

Rodger Campbell is my big brother, coach, mentor, business partner, and friend. His constant prodding is one of the reasons I wrote this book. Thank you, *Doctor Campbell,* for providing me with the medicine to be *Sum Thing Else.*

Scott Cummings in my best friend and someone I truly look up to. He is a role model who provides me with constant encouragement. Thank you, *Skillz,* for always being there for the good times and the not so good times.

Jim Gordon III is my brother and one-man technology help desk. *Jim Jim*, thank you for sharing my information with everyone in cyberspace and being my tech guru.

Melissa Kitchen is my sister and Ms. Honesty. I know that I can always go to her for an honest opinion. She has always believed in me and given me great ideas and advice. Thank you, *Mimi;* you are an amazing woman. Your passion always inspires me.

Tony Marino, Teresa Whittaker, Amber Walters, and the rest of my Ohio friends have always treated me like family. Thank you for keeping my head on straight.

Edie Mack is my mom. She is the reason that I am the man I am today. She is a teacher in real life, and my teacher for life. Thank you, Mom, for teaching me everything you know! Many of the ideas I am sharing in this book were ideas you first planted in me.

Writing this book has been an amazing experience. I truly hope you enjoy the stories inside.

Frank Kitchen

CHAPTER 1

WHY ARE YOU WRITING A BOOK?

A blog is defined as a website written by an individual or group of users to produce an ongoing narrative. It comes from the words web and log.

A book is defined as a written piece of work consisting of pages glued or sewn together and bound by a cover.

Throughout my life, people have told me I should write a book to share my adventures and knowledge. I thought that it was weird, considering I have no formal journalistic training. I wasn't an avid reader of books. I wasn't a fan of writing long papers in school. How was I going to write a book?

My mom made me read a lot as a child. She signed me up for the *Weekly Reader Book Club*. Every week, a new book came in the mail. I read the ones that I liked, while many went unread. As I got older, my reading encompassed comic books, the world atlas, history books, magazines, journals, advertisements, websites, and lots of office paperwork.

I loved to talk, but writing a book seemed impossible to me. Then, I graduated college and entered the professional workplace. I needed to share my thoughts with others when I couldn't share them verbally. I started writing newsletters. It was an easy and fun way to share important information. I could put my thoughts together in a clear and concise way. I could be direct and to the point without writing a book.

In the summer of 2005, my family moved to Florida. I wanted them to keep up to date with my life and thoughts. That's when I was introduced to the world of blogging. A friend showed me how to set up my own site. Soon, I was posting stories and pictures of my life's ups and downs. My family and friends could see what I was up to. I named my blog "Fresh from the Kitchen." Every entry was a fresh idea that I could share with the people close to me. Before I knew it, people I didn't know were reading my blog.

People enjoyed my thoughts and ideas on a variety of subjects. They were sharing them with their family and friends. I wrote a blog while I was in Australia and discovered that people were reading my blog daily with their morning coffee. There were people who sent me concerned e-mails when I didn't blog for an extended period of time. There were even more people who commented that I should write a book.

I told myself that I didn't have time to write a book. I made excuses about being too busy. I was too busy living life and sharing the stories on my blog. One night while uploading a new blog entry, I began reading my past entries. There were over 600 entries to sort through. I discovered that I had enough material to write several books.

That is the night my idea light bulb lit up: *write your book like you write your blogs! Write a narrative of stories bound by a cover.* People write books for many reasons. My reason is simple: I would like to share stories that will educate, inspire and entertain people about life and leadership.

To read my blog, please go to www.kitchenfrank.com.

CHAPTER 2

CELEBRATE LIFE

~~~~~~~

"Life is about experiences and relationships!" – Bernie Morgan

In 2006, I was sitting in the home of Bernie Morgan in Adelaide, Australia. I was having an insightful conversation with Bernie, his wife Colleen, and my friend Dave. We discussed politics, religion, family, friends, food, and wine. While sipping a glass of wine, Bernie made the quote that has changed my life. *Life is about experiences and relationships.*

I was in Australia for the adventure of a lifetime. Six weeks exploring the country as representative for Rotary International and the United States. Bernie and his wife Colleen were hosting my friend Dave and I. As our host family, they taught us about their country and culture. Bernie and Colleen aren't big fans of television. They are big fans of developing strong relationships and creating lasting memories. The week that I spent with them was amazing.

Time spent with Bernie and Colleen was all about people. It was about learning and communication. It was about experiences. One of my experiences took place on Easter Sunday. Bernie took our group to a hanger at a small airfield. The hanger belonged to a friend who collected vintage aircraft. One of his prized planes was a World War I United States Army biplane. Our group of three each had the opportunity to fly in the plane. I was the last person to fly in the open cockpit plane. The weather was perfect, the views were amazing, and the experience is permanently etched in my mind and the memory card of my digital camera.

Reliving that story made me realize that I have an amazing life. I've accomplished more than I could have imagined. I have been told my stories and experiences are inspiring. Truth be told, they inspire me too. They give me the urge to pursue new experiences and to continue to develop positive relationships. The stories of these experiences and relationships will be shared with you in this book.

Amazing experiences are the offspring of strong and positive relationships. You too have lived an amazing life. You have accomplished the unthinkable. Your experiences can inspire the people around you. They will inspire you to do more in the future. Life is a celebration. Make time to relive your accomplishments. Dedicate time to develop and nurture relationships. Make the most out of every experience. And, remember to celebrate! Thank you, Bernie and Colleen, for a very important life lesson and your continued friendship.

CHAPTER 3

INSPIRATION

~~~~~~~~~~

"Really great people make you feel that you, too can become great."

– Mark Twain

I worked at Lakeland Community College in Kirtland, Ohio for nine years. I left the school in July of 2007 to pursue a career as a professional speaker, and to move closer to my future wife in Arizona. Many of my co-workers told me that they would miss me.

I informed the college of my decision to leave that May. Every week, the President of the college sent out a letter to the employees. The letters covered a variety of subjects. That May, he asked college employees to contribute to the weekly letter. When word of my departure spread, he asked me to write something. Here's what I wrote. This is one of the *light bulb* moments that made me write this book.

(May 2007)

I received a phone call last week from the President's Office "asking" me if I would write the next edition of "Morris' Musings." My options were "yes" or "yes." I decided on option number two. Once I committed myself to be this week's "Special Guest Writer," I needed something to write about. Should I write something serious? Should I be funny? Should I keep it short? Hmmmm? Then it hit me: I'm going to do what I do best, I'm going to be me! First step, name my musing. "Fresh from the Kitchen." Next step, start typing.

"Fresh from the Kitchen" Edition #1

Friday, July 20, 2007 will be my last day of employment at Lakeland Community College. My experiences at Lakeland have been amazing. I often tell people that I might have to write a book or a sitcom about some of the experiences. We often refer to the people who work here as "The Lakeland Family." I would like to thank that family for taking me in. I especially want to thank Rich Novotny for taking the chance to hire and mentor an inexperienced kid nine years ago.

That leads me to my musing. I would like to thank Morris for inviting me to write to all of you. I also want to thank Morris in advance for the Clocktower Award presented to me for all my hard work on this musing (hint, hint). I've been reading Morris' Musings since he started writing them. At the end of every musing, he thanks everyone for Impacting Lives through Learning. I often think to myself, what does that mean? "Impacting Lives through Learning" is Lakeland's slogan. It's Lakeland core purpose. Do we think about this core purpose every time we come to Lakeland?

In December of 1991, I moved to Mentor, Ohio from Philadelphia, Pennsylvania. I had the grades, several college acceptance letters, but not enough money to go to the "REAL" colleges. My mom suggested I enroll at Lakeland Community College. I was a little hesitant at first. I didn't want to go to a "community college"! I will admit, I was very young and very misinformed about community colleges. In 1992, I started taking classes at Lakeland. I soon discovered how much of an impact Lakeland would have on my life.

Impact is defined as a significant or strong influence. It is also defined as the effect something has on something else. This influence or effect can be positive or negative. In my case, the impact was very positive. As a student, Lakeland offered affordable classes taught by top-notch instructors. Lakeland also offered a variety of co-curricular opportunities to help me grow personally outside the classroom. That combination turned a shy kid into an outgoing young adult with a two-year Associates Degree in 1995.

I eventually transferred to the University of Akron, then went on to Myers University. Then, I got my first job in the real world. At school or at work, I was often asked, "where did you learn that?" I always replied, "Lakeland Community College." I started to recognize how much of an impact Lakeland had on my life. It was more personal than the real schools. I could talk to someone face to face when I needed help or assistance. I learned skills for the classroom, and skills for life, from the people at Lakeland.

I eventually came back to Lakeland in 1998 to work in the Student Activities Office. What a great opportunity and experience! I wanted to share the positive experiences that I had as a Lakeland student with current students. Many students and their parents tell me about the positive impact Lakeland and I had on their lives. Many of those students don't realize the impact they have on my life and our lives. They help us as we continue to learn and grow.

Fifteen years after I first stepped foot on the Lakeland campus, I am preparing to leave again. I'm preparing to take on the new challenge of living in a new state, developing new relationships and pursuing new career opportunities. I start to think what got me to this point and once again I know its Lakeland. There is a statement: "you never know what you have until it's gone." Soon Lakeland will be a memory, but I'll always remember my time here.

Being in a learning environment is motivating. Everyone has a dream. Everyone wants to take on the world in some way. Lakeland is a stepping-stone for students to achieve their dreams. The faculty and staff at Lakeland have a strong influence on students achieving their dreams. We are the "something" affecting "something" else.

We are all here because of the students. Without the students, we wouldn't have our jobs. Every time a student or prospective student comes in contact with a member of the Lakeland Family, we are impacting their lives. Learning doesn't only happen in the classroom, it happens everywhere on campus. We need to think about how we can impact the lives of the students and our Lakeland Family members in a positive way

Do you know who's who on campus? Do you know the responsibilities of the different departments? If you see trash around campus, do you pick it up? Do you answer your phone or let it go into voicemail? Do you complain about everything or make suggestions for improvement? Do you respond quickly to your e-mails? Do you help mentor new college employees? Do you attend campus events or programs? Do you take advantage of the classes offered? Do you share your Lakeland stories with students and co-workers? The list goes on and on. All are examples of experiences that impact people (students and employees) on campus. We have the choice to make it a positive or negative experience. That choice impacts the lives of many people: prospective students, current students, and employees.

Lakeland has used the slogans "Students First," "Opportunity Starts Here," and currently "Impacting Lives through Learning." These words focus on the number one thing at Lakeland: the students. Lakeland and its employees have had a positive impact on thousands of students/people. I am one of them. In turn, I have positively impacted the lives of others. It's easy to focus on the negative, but we should take the time to focus on the positive impact we can make. The next time you read Morris's Musing and you see the term "Impacting Lives through Learning," think about that new student stepping on campus for the first time or that student crossing stage at graduation. Think about what you do here at Lakeland. Ask yourself: "Does my attitude or work make a negative impact on that life or a positive impact?" I hope all of you go for option number two!

Thank you, Lakeland,

Frank Kitchen

A few days later, I received this e-mail:

Frank,

It looks like you may be on to something here. You could start by simply doing a personal journal. Then, after a few years, you could publish your writings and retire a wealthy and young man. Then, you could come back here and be President. Just something to think about. Thanks again, Frank. I would say your Kitchen Musing was very well-received.

Morris

CHAPTER 4

THE KITCHEN SINK THEORY

~~~~~~~~~~~

"You're not finished making a meal until all the dishes are clean."
- Mrs. Thompson – My High School Home Economics Teacher

I participated in cooking classes for three years in high school. I heard countless jokes about my last name and participating voluntarily in the classes. I made a lot of friends on the school bus when I brought my tasty creations home. Things went so well that my teacher suggested that I attend a cooking school after I graduated. Many of the themes I learned in my classes that I still use today.

One of the most important themes taught in the class was to keep our work areas clean. This meant we needed to wash our dishes and cooking utensils as soon as possible. Whether a meal was cooking on the stovetop or baking in the oven, we were taught to clean the dirty cookware while preparing the meal. Our teacher told us this would save us time and make things a lot easier. This was very true. By the time the meal was ready to eat, we didn't have any dishes to clean. Our workspaces were clean and the only things left to clean were the dishes we ate from.

I want you to do the following right now:

1. **Get up from your reading location and take this book to your kitchen.**

2. **Survey your kitchen sink.**

3. **Return to your previous reading location and continue reading.**

What did the sink look like? Was it full of dirty dishes? Could you find your silverware hidden under the plates? Were there any pots or pans with the left over residue from the last meal you cooked? Gross! Did you see any glasses or bowls with mysterious liquids in them? Yuck! Did you look at all the sink and say, "I don't have time to clean all these dishes."

Life can be the same way. Dirty dishes are the unfinished projects that you started and didn't complete. You need to complete your projects before you start your next one. Unfinished projects build up until they overwhelm you. A pile of dirty dishes is very overwhelming. The way your kitchen sink looks is reflection of your life. This is the *Kitchen Sink Theory.*

The dishwasher was invented to relieve you of the burden of washing dishes. When dishes pile up, you put them in the dishwasher and the machine does all the work for you. Unfortunately, life doesn't work same way. Some people have dishwashers and some don't. Do you have a dishwasher?

In this fast-paced world, everyone is busy. We have limited free time to enjoy life. The same can be said about cooking. Making the meal is fun. Eating the meal is enjoyable. Cleaning up afterwards is unstimulating, but a major part of the process. My cooking classes taught me that it was easier to wash the dishes as I worked. The classes taught me to finish my projects.

Until you clean the dishes in your sink the meal you just made is not complete. You will have a tough time preparing your next culinary masterpiece if the dishes you need are dirty. Letting projects build up eats away at your valuable and limited free time.

The key is to stay on stop of things. Don't let one unfinished project after another build up. If you're letting the dishes in your sink build up, look at your life. Ask yourself the following questions:

1. **Am I letting projects on my *to-do list* go unfinished or unstarted?**
2. **Am I constantly saying, "I'll get to it later?"**
3. **Do I wait to begin projects until I *have* to do them?**
4. **Do I wait to clean my dishes until I have no dishes to eat from?**

If you answered yes to any of these questions, then it's time for you to start cleaning the dishes in your sink. Take the time to clean your dishes as you cook. The five minutes it takes to clean them now is a lot less than the twenty minutes it will take you later. Cleaning dishes as you go will make your life easier.

No matter what your next dream project is, be sure to tackle it in small manageable amounts. If you wait too long, your dream may appear impossible. Good luck staying on top of your dishes! Keep your kitchen clean, because a clean kitchen will inspire you to create the recipes of your dreams.

CHAPTER 5

ARE YOU AN APPLE PICKER?

"Life is the sum of all your choices."

- Albert Camus

Anything you want to do in life is like picking apples. You can pick apples from a tree, you can pick them from a display of apples at a store or market, or you can buy them by the bag. Of course, you can also choose not to get any at all. The thing is that, no matter where you pick your apples, there are different types of right and wrong. Apples can be just right, not ready yet, too ripe, bruised, or rotten.

There are people who pick their own apples, and there are people who have other people pick the apples for them. There are those who just wait for them to fall from the tree. Some don't do anything at all. I want to be the person who picks his own apples.

By picking my own apples, a lot can happen.

1. I will have a great selection to pick from. I can pick one or I can pick many. Some will be just right while others may need time to ripen. I'll have the ability to avoid the rotten ones. The key is that I will have multiple options!
2. I won't have to worry about someone keeping all the best apples for themselves.
3. I will have a good feeling inside knowing that I made something happen.
4. I will gain knowledge and experiences that I can use for future apple picking.

Picking apples is hard work. I may have to climb a tree, drag a ladder to the tree, find a cherry picker, knock the tree over, or simply go to the store. I will need help along the way from other apple pickers, too. My hard work will pay off. I will learn how to be assertive. I will learn how to take advantage of opportunities. I will learn not to wait around for something to happen!

I hope you choose to be an apple picker, too! Don't be the person waiting for the apples to fall out of a tree. You never know what you might get. If you pick an apple or two, don't wait too long to enjoy it. It may begin to rot if you wait too long.

It's time for me to wrap up this chapter of the book; I've got apples to pick. For the other apple pickers in my life, thank you for sharing the knowledge of what to look for, encouraging me to pursue my passions, and showing me how to climb the tree, or where to find a ladder. I plan on picking a lot of apples, and I plan on sharing them with my family, friends, and people I spend time with. Life is short. Pick your apples and don't let them get old or rotten.

CHAPTER 6

HAVE YOU LOST YOUR CREATIVITY?

"Creativity is inventing, experimenting, growing, taking risks, breaking rules, making mistakes, and having fun."

- Mary Lou Cook

Everyone participates in activities that require passion and creativity to make them materialize. Dreams don't become reality by following the status quo. Life is short, and there are a ton of activities we want to pursue.

One Spring, I was doing my spring cleaning when I came across an old sketchpad and art supplies. I also found old photos I took for a photography class. Great memories filled my head. Questions populated my head, too. I wondered, "am I as creative as I used to be?"

The answer was yes and no. I remembered the day that I drew a picture at work to welcome people to our office. Most people were surprised that I drew the picture. I grew up drawing all of the time. I turned the visions in my head into reality on paper. Years later, I surprised people by drawing monthly pictures on the information board in my office. There are times that I am creative in my life, but was I being creative all the time? I didn't think that I was, but doing my spring cleaning definitely rekindled my creative juices.

I became a kid again. Kids enjoy life. As adults, our lives can become routine. We neglect opportunities to enjoy the little things. We don't take time to laugh, explore, ask questions, dream, or create. Spring cleaning helped me discover something: the more I use my creativity, the

...... I enjoy life. Life is less boring when I make the most out of every opportunity.

I started writing down all of the things that I dreamt of doing. I amazed myself with all the ideas I came up with. I had ideas for the people close to me and for myself. I was working at Lakeland Community College. I was responsible for assisting students achieve their dreams. They came to me for ideas and I used my creativity to aid them, but what was I doing for me?

I decided to take my own advice: life isn't all about your job. Pursue activities you are truly passionate about and be creative with everything you do. Take the time to rediscover your past so you can truly appreciate the present and create the future you desire.

CHAPTER 7

NEW YEAR'S RESOLUTIONS

"What is not started today is never finished tomorrow."
- Johann Wolfgang von Goethe

At the end of every year, people start making New Year's resolutions. I researched the definition. All the definitions that I researched sounded like goals to me. Call it a semantics thing, but I like to make New Year's Goals. I'm definitely a goal-oriented person. I like having something to shoot for. You can call it a resolution, goal, oath, promise, decree, declaration, or pledge. Be sure to share the information with the people closest to you.

One summer, I started meeting with a good friend, Kyle. We met to share our personal and professional goals. We also shared information to help us achieve our goals. Every time we met, the pressure was on to prove we were working on our goals. When Kyle and his wife moved away, we kept in touch through e-mail. I wrote to check on him and he thanked me for reminding him about his goals.

One morning, I opened an e-mail from Kyle. He asked me how I was doing with my goals. I thanked him for the small push. I set many goals that summer and I'm proud to say I met or surpassed most of them. I didn't recognize this until I wrote him to give him my progress report.

While typing my report, I started to think about that year. I always plan for the year to be better year than my previous one. I realized that it's hard to achieve your goals if you don't share them with the people who are close to you. I read a book called *Get off your Butt and Do it*

Now by Jermaine M. Davis. The author talks about developing a team to support you. Goals are dreams. Your support team makes it possible for your dreams to come true. Your support group should consist of people you trust, people who will push and support you during your endeavors. I developed a strong team. By sharing my goals, I had double pressure. If I didn't pursue my goals, I would be letting myself down, and let my team down. I truly believe that you cannot reach your goals if you keep them inside. If you're proud of something, you have to share it with other people. This can be verbal or visual; the key is to share.

When you are thinking about your next set of New Year's resolutions, be sure to think about the people you will share your resolution with. Create a name for them and let them know you're asking for their assistance with your resolutions. Type or write out your resolutions and put them somewhere you can see them. Give that list to your team and ask them to remind you or help you with your resolutions. Who knows, they may ask you to do the same thing for them. It's amazing what you can achieve when you have constant reminders. Remember: "out of sight, out of mind." Good luck to everyone! Think positive, and turn those resolutions into reality.

Are you ready to create your *support team*? The time is now. Please use a separate piece of paper or a journal to put your team together. Write down their name, birthday, address, e-mail, phone number, and why you want them on your team. These people will assist you in making your dreams come true. Your entry should look like this:

_____'s Support Team

Name:
Birthday:
Address:
 E-mail:
Phone Number:
What makes them special?

CHAPTER 8

RESOLUTIONS VERSUS GOALS

~~~~~~

*"Set a goal and follow through. The world is full of unachieved
yet reachable goals! Never give up!"*

– Unknown

Resolution: a firm decision to do or not to do something.

Goals: the object of a person's ambition or effort; an aim or desired
result.

Action Steps: a measure or action, esp. one of a series taken in order to
deal with or achieve a particular thing.

New Year's Eve is a time of excitement. People around the world
celebrate the beginning of a new year. The New Year provides a clean
slate. It's a time to devise resolutions that will produce an extraordinary
year.

Every New Year's Eve, I'm presented with the same question: "what
are your resolutions for the New Year?" My answer always results in
dumbfounded looks: "I don't make resolutions!" I tell them that I make
goals with action steps. They give me a confused look, and ask me what
the difference is.

Look at the definition above. A resolution is the decision to do
something. There isn't any action there. Making a goal means your
ambitions and desires are one step closer to becoming reality. Goals can
be measured. Goals need to be written down. The next course of action
is to write down the steps needed to achieve your goals. The goals and
action steps have to be measurable.

Many people tell me they want to lose weight during the New Year. This is their New Year's resolution. They never state how much weight they want to lose or give a time line for losing the weight. Good goals have measurable objectives, a timeline, and actions steps.

Here is an example: an individual weighs 200 pounds. They make a resolution to lose weight in the New Year. At the end of the year, they weigh 199 pounds. They have successfully accomplished their resolution, but are disappointed because they wanted to weigh 175 pounds. They made a resolution, not a goal. With a clearly defined objective and action plan, the chances of achieving a goal increase immensely.

There's nothing wrong with making a resolution, but people say a lot of things they never do. I talk a lot, and dream a lot too. The way that I challenge myself to achieve my dreams is to create a plan. To take this a step further, I send my goals and action steps to my closest friends. My success team is there to offer support, knowledge, experience, and friendship. They are there to kick my butt when I slack off, too!

I wish everyone the best of luck as you achieve your resolutions and goals. Remember this: goal setting is like grocery shopping. You can say that you need to go shopping, but if you don't make a list, you always end up forgetting something important.

CHAPTER 9

WHAT'S ON YOUR GROCERY LIST?

"It must be borne in mind that the tragedy of life doesn't lie in not reaching your goal. The tragedy lies in having no goal to reach."

- Benjamin E. Mays

Life is all about wants and needs. There are many things we need and even more things we want. In short, life is like shopping at the grocery store.

When you go shopping, you will see many things that you need and want. People are very visual. Without a list, you can become distracted easily. Stores are designed to appeal to your visual stimuli. Many of these stimuli are on your grocery list. As you shop, you determine what fits into your current budget and schedule. The important factor is to have the items on a list so you don't forget them. If you don't get them this week, you'll get them in the future.

Some people don't shop with a list, and they end up buying what they don't need, what they don't want, or something they have too many of. Does this sound like your life?

Many of us don't have a "life grocery list." This is a list of dreams. What do you need in life, and what do you want? It is amazing to see what you really want and need out of life when you write it down. My challenge to you is to take a couple of sheets of paper and a couple of hours alone to write or draw everything you want and need in life. There is no limit to what you write. This is a list you can work on for the rest of your life. Some people may complete their lists faster than others. Just remember: this is your grocery list. You can always add items to the list as you think about them. As you complete an item on your list, cross it out. As you start to cross items out, you will experience the feeling of accomplishment. You may not be able to cross many of the items off the list now, but you can always go back to the list to remember what you wrote down.   A goal is a dream with a plan. Without a dream, there are no goals!

If you don't write down what you want and need in life, then remember the old statement: "out of sight, out of mind." Writing down your dreams is the first step to achieving them. Reviewing your dreams will inspire you to complete the ones you haven't crossed off your list.

> *"Your future hasn't been written yet. No one's has. Your future is whatever you make it. So make it a good one."*
> *- Doc Brown – Back to the Future Series*

No matter your age, it is never too early, or too late, to make a grocery list. You can always add more to your grocery list. It is never too late to add items to your grocery list. Grab a piece of paper and get started. Go ahead, start now, before you read the next chapter. I've included one of my grocery lists to provide you with a little inspiration.

FRANK KITCHEN'S GROCERY LIST:

December 15, 2014

1. To be the best husband I can possibly be
2. To be the best father I can possibly be
3. To be debt free by the age of 43
4. To write and publish a children's book
5. To shoot under 80 for 18 holes of golf
6. To attend the Olympic games
7. To compete in and complete a triathlon
8. To ride in a hot air balloon
9. To celebrate New Year's Eve in New York City
10. To visit all seven continents
11. To go white water rafting
12. To read the bible
13. To take my wife to Australia
14. To be a travel writer/host
15. To be fluent in Spanish
16. To visit my birthplace in Germany
17. To assist my wife with her dream to be a business owner
18. To run a full marathon in under 5 hours
19. To visit the Great Wall of China
20. To give the commencement speeches at the high school and college I attended
21. To own a house
22. To take dance lessons with my wife
23. To save over $2 million
24. To speak in all 50 United States
25. To take my family on an amazing family vacation

CHAPTER 10

MOTIVATIONAL POEM

〜〜〜〜〜

"*Poetry is when an emotion has found its thought and the thought has found words.*"

- Robert Frost

I was removing old files from my computer when came across a poem I wrote during a moment of creativity. I would love to share it with you.

There's a Nike slogan that we all know: "just do it!" Life is short and this slogan is effective. That is the reason I wrote this poem, because the slogan puts me in a mood.

Just Do It!

You know what you want; you wonder if you can do it? Do you do the safe thing or do you go for what's really calling you? You don't know who to listen to: your mind, your heart or the people close to you? You want to be happy, but how much will it cost you? You only live once and you rarely get second chances. You'll kick yourself later if you don't just do it! If you really want what's going to make you happy, you better just do it or you'll sit there stewing. Do your thing and listen to the song from your heart. Nothing happens when you sit around. Open yourself to new experiences, you never know until you try. Have the courage to do it. Get into action; take a step forward and do like Nike says and "Just Do It!"

CHAPTER 11

WITH DREAMS COME PLANS

"If you fail to plan, then you plan to fail." – Unknown

Have you ever watched a political debate? The politicians offer advice and tell people what needs to be done. It's tough to believe in politicians when you find out they are doing the opposite of what they preach. If you take a minute to reflect, many of the politicians sound just like us.

During the United States Presidential election of 2008, I began to think about the comments that I make to people. We often hear the political candidates go back and forth about their dreams for the community. We hear about what they will do when they get into office. The candidates all have dreams.

Dreams are nice, but people want to know: is there a plan? Yes, we can go to a political website to learn more, but people want to hear more of what you are going to do versus what you would like to do.

As humorous as this may sound, we are just like the people running for political office. We talk about our dreams. We talk about what we would do if "x" happens. But just like the candidates and politicians, we don't talk about our plans. Dreams are defined the following ways:

1. A series of thoughts, images and sensations occurring in a person's mind.

2. A cherished aspiration, ambition or ideal.

3. An unrealistic or self-deluding fantasy.

People want reality, not dreams. Do you waste a lot of time and energy just dreaming? Are you focused on the wrong thing? Do you get distracted easily? Dreaming is a wonderful thing. A world without dreamers would be a boring place. The key is to use some of your valuable time and energy to plan it out after you dream it. Dreams do not magically come true. Plans and actions make dreams come true. You have to make your dreams turn into reality.

I'm sure that you are thinking, *dreams are fun and plans are boring!* Yes, it's true that plans are no fun. Experiencing a dream come true is a lot fun. Remember, all successful people have a plan to make their dreams become reality. They share their dreams and plans with supportive people. You can call them boring, but they are having fun. They are enjoying life while dreamers are simply dreaming about having fun.

Good luck as you turn your dreams into reality. It's nice to talk about dreams, but it is more fun to see them become reality.

I'll end this chapter with a classic line from a television show from the 1980s, something I would like you to practice saying:

"I love it when a plan comes together!" – *The A-Team*

CHAPTER 12

DO YOU HAVE A SOUNDTRACK?

"Play some good tunes." – Anthony Marino

In my 20s, Friday nights were the nights I went out with my friends. Most Fridays were spent with my friend Tony. It didn't matter what we did as long as we were together. No matter who drove, I knew what Tony would say: "play some good tunes." Tony loved music. The music that we played in the car put us in a good mood. The better the music, the better the experience.

"Listening to music can decrease your stress hormones by 20%."
- Livestrong.com

Music has to be one of the most influential creations of mankind. No matter the genre, music has the amazing ability to spark memories, emotions, and behaviors. People spend a lot of time watching television. In 2014, *The New York Daily News* reported that the average American watched 35 hours of television every week. My question is how much television do people really remember?

Music, however, can bring back memories of a specific date or time instantly. While writing this book, I listened to music.

One day I was going through some boxes and found CDs that Tony had made for me. Almost every weekend, he would put together a new *Marino Mix* to get us energized before we went out. I remember him constantly playing the soundtrack from the *Rocky* movies. I played one of Tony's CDs and good memories filled my head. It was as if I were listening to the soundtrack of my twenties. I started to remember funny moments. I could remember exactly where I first heard a song. In many cases, I could remember who I was with when I heard the song. Music is incredible.

Do you listen to music? What do you listen to? My musical taste varies. I have learned to pay attention to the lyrics and instruments. The talent that it takes to master an instrument is remarkable. Song lyrics contain words that can inspire and motivate.

Music can be the catalyst for positive experiences. Charles F. Emory of *The Ohio State University* reported that music increased a person's ability to organize cognitive output. No matter the music played during his study, participants reported feeling better emotionally and mentally after working out with music, versus no music.

I'm not a scientist, but I know that music makes me more productive. If I'm in the house cleaning, I work more efficiently when I have music on. Music gives me ideas when I'm brainstorming ideas for speeches. Music puts me in the right mood before I go onstage. Music adds so much to our lives. It can provide the theme for a high school dance. Music is used to set the mood and tone of movies. It gets people's attention when played at the beginning of a wedding. It is played at important events and ceremonies. Simply put, music is the soundtrack of our life.

I want you to be as productive as possible. The best way to do this is to compile a personal soundtrack. If your life were a movie and it had a soundtrack, what songs would you choose?

On a piece of paper, write down fifteen song titles with the artist's name. This is your personal soundtrack. This soundtrack will consist of the songs that inspire and motivate you to do your best, to never quit, to do the unthinkable. Save this soundtrack on whatever device you listen to music with. Can you hear the songs in your head right now? Do you feel that smile coming on your face? Can you sense the energy body? This is what music does to us. It is the feeling of liste tunes.

Your list should look like this:

_____'s Personal Soundtrack

	Name	Artist
1.		
2.		
3.		
4.		
5.		
6.		
7.		
8.		
9.		
10.		
11.		
12.		
13.		
14.		
15.		

CHAPTER 13

A LITTLE EXTRA EFFORT GOES A LONG WAY!

"Giving that extra degree makes all the difference."
— *Drew Brees, NFL Quarterback*

There are moments in our lives where we become inspired to achieve, attempt, or pursue an aspiration, to hope or dream. Movies can inspire us, people can inspire us, books can inspire us, and various forms of social media can inspire us. I am inspired by great conversations with co-workers, students, friends, and family. Conversations can be very motivating.

I love to hear stories of people achieving the impossible. When I hear these stories, it makes me think of all the things I can do. Here is the amazing story of my friend Katie Spotz.

Attending a college or university can cost an unthinkable amount of money. The price tag can strike fear in a lot of people. The total cost can cause prospective students to give up on their dream of obtaining a college education. There are many ways to find the money to pay for a college degree, but most people don't know where to look. They don't believe that there is money available. They don't do the research, or ask questions. Many just quit and join the work force. The courageous ones look in the mirror and take action. They lead and motivate themselves toward achieving their dream. Their determination keeps their enthusiasm alive.

My friend Katie faced this very situation when it came time to attend college. She had good grades, but her family didn't have the money to pay for the school she wanted to attend. She discussed her dream of getting her college degree with several friends. They suggested she apply for scholarships and grants. She didn't know much about the pots of free money available to prospective college students.

She began to ask questions of people with knowledge on the subject. The answers that she received excited her. She began to spend much her free time researching grants and scholarships. She discovered that she would have to fill out long applications, write longer essays, collect letters of recommendation, and in some cases, be interviewed face to face. All these barriers make most people quit, but not Katie. She was determined to find the money to pay for her education.

Katie endured many failures. She applied for over thirty different grants and scholarships. Many organizations she applied to had never responded. That just made her more determined to apply for more scholarships. Each time she applied, she needed more letters of recommendation. I was one of the letter writers, so I quickly became invested in her dream. Many of the organizations she applied to, I never heard of. More than two-thirds declined her applications. Many would consider this a failure, but Katie was happy. Several of the grants and scholarships were approved. None of them were for huge amounts of money, but when they were all added together, I was amazed when I found out her entire education was paid for.

This experience only increased Katie's confidence. She has pursued amazing opportunities. As I write, her list of achievements continues to grow. She has participated in educational programs and community service projects in North Carolina, California, Australia, New Zealand, and Thailand. She received her college degree. She completed a three thousand mile bike ride to raise money for the *American Lung Association.* She even rowed a boat across the Atlantic Ocean to raise money for the *Blue Planet Run Foundation.* It is amazing what Katie's determination has done. All this started when Katie put in the extra effort to chase her dreams of obtaining a college education. I'll bet that you and I both would be equally amazed at what our determination can produce.

For more information on Katie and her amazing adventures, please look her up on the internet or her website: www.katiespotz.com

CHAPTER 14

GET COMFORTABLE BEING UNCOMFORTABLE

"You need to be comfortable being uncomfortable."

- Dr. Bernard Franklin

I truly didn't understand the quote above until one fateful day. I'm always told how well I relate to new people and situations. I put those comments to the test when I visited a local meeting of *Rotary International*. I wanted to learn more about the organization. I also wanted to introduce myself to the organization's leadership and members. Rotary was about to send me with four other professionals to Australia as a part of their Group Study Exchange Program (GSE). I was asked to spend four weeks in a foreign country as an ambassador and representative of Northeast Ohio. Meeting the people I would be representing was a logical decision.

When I arrived for the meeting, I introduced myself to their President. The next thing that I knew, I was on the agenda speaking to a room full of local business and civic leaders. My heart was beating a million times an hour. Once I got to the front of the room, and was handed the microphone, things changed. I smile when I think how I was truly comfortable in an uncomfortable situation.

I was comfortable because I took Dr. Franklin's advice. I saw this as a new challenge and great preparation for my trip to Australia. Before I knew it, my time was done. I had introduced myself to a room full of strangers. I had fully explained why I was there and what the trip was about. I answered questions. After the meeting, several people came up to congratulate me and tell me how well I had spoken in front of a group.

They invited me to come back and speak again. I was asked to speak to other organizations.

A few minutes before things started, I was nervous and had no clue what I was going to say; I took a deep breath and the rest is history. It is important that you never let them see you sweat. I took an uncomfortable situation and made it into a comfortable one. This was the beginning of my speaking career.

That day was a great experience. It was also a great example of what I was taught years before: "be comfortable being uncomfortable." We are always going to experience new, nerve-racking situations. You need to take the new situation as a personal challenge; tackle new situations and build upon them. Your new experiences become past experiences that you have learned from. Every new experience in your life is an opportunity for growth. I confidently know that I can go into a room full of strangers and perform on the spot. Life is all about experiences. Some of them may be uncomfortable, but you'll have some great stories to share once you tackle them.

To learn more about Rotary International and the Group Study Exchange program, go to: **www.Rotary.org**.

CHAPTER 15

LIFE AND DEATH

〰〰〰

"Dream as if you'll live forever, live as if you'll die today."

- James Dean

The death of a loved one is never easy. I've had several people close to me lose a loved one. Some were expected and others were unexpected. When a death happens, what do you say to put one's mind at ease? If I were in their shoes, would I want my loved one to pass away unexpectedly, or would I want to know exactly when things would end?

I started thinking about death when I had to have my living will and durable power of attorney notarized for a trip outside of the country. It's scary to think that I was preparing for my eventual death, but I also felt good that the people closest to me would know what to do when that day happens. They would know what my wishes were. We hear so many stories of people suddenly dying and no one knowing what to do; hearing these stories really got me thinking about my will.

While I was preparing my will, I heard a story of a U.S. serviceman who passed away in Iraq. He had been writing his family constantly via e-mail. Due to privacy laws, the family was unable to get into his e-mail account to collect the e-mails that they had exchanged. After six months of non-usage, the e-mail account was deleted. It made me think, "do the people closest to me know where I keep my important information?" and "do they I know what my wishes are if I were to pass away unexpectedly?"

I began to put together an emergency file on my computer. I started collecting all my passwords for everything, all of my account information, phone numbers, and contact information of my friends and family. I put together lists of where to find things in my apartment. All of my planning helped me realize how much the people closest to me didn't know about me. It was scary. I thought about how tough things would really be if I had passed away. Death isn't an easy thing, but I'd like it to be somewhat easier for the people closest to me. After I completed my list, I made copies. I gave them to the people that I trust.

The copies were put into envelopes that said "open in case of an emergency." My mind was at ease because I knew my family and friends wouldn't be on the news fighting with the government or a hospital because no one knew what to do.

I hope that I didn't scare you. I wrote this as a reflection piece. Do the people closest to you really know you? Do you really know the people closest to you? What are your wishes in case there is an unexpected emergency? There are a lot of businesses that have an emergency plan. Do you and your loved ones have one?

In loving memory of Richard A. Cummings
June 9, 1938 –October 12, 2009

CHAPTER 16

DO YOU HAVE A MISSION STATEMENT?

"You have to have a goal to reach it." - Scott Cummings

I am invited to speak at conferences and workshops worldwide. I'll admit that it's a cool career. I get to give organizations and businesses advice on how to improve themselves both personally and professionally. I talk about setting goals and discovering their purpose. The people that I work with constantly provide me with great feedback, comments, and ideas.

Their comments get me thinking: I am a goal-oriented person. I always set goals for myself, but I wasn't setting my goals with a main purpose in mind. Life is a marathon, but I'd been training for short races. I decided to make a personal mission statement for myself. I needed to set a goal for the race called life.

Here's what I came up with. It's my mission statement with objectives on how to accomplish my mission.

The Mission Statement of Frank Cornelius Kitchen

The mission for Frank Cornelius Kitchen is to live a life full of positive experiences. My mission will be achieved by constantly pursuing the following goals.

1. 1. Sharing my dreams, goals, feelings, and thoughts with people close to me.
2. Dealing with others with honesty, integrity, tolerance, compassion and respect.
3. Sharing, teaching and coaching what I've learned.
4. Having a positive influence on the people that I come in contact with.
5. Making life fun and enjoyable.
6. Practicing what I preach.
7. Showing financially responsibility.
8. Capitalizing on opportunities to learn, improve and educate myself.
9. Taking care of myself physically.
10. Putting myself in positive situations and environments.
11. Traveling as much as possible.
12. Being open, and respectful to new ideas and experiences.

I've shared my mission statement with you; what is your mission statement and whom will you share it with? Get started now on by writing you mission statement on a piece of paper.

CHAPTER 17

ARE YOU A B.A.D. A.P.P.L.E.?

~~~~~~~~~~~~~~~~~~~~~

"B.A.D. is a way of Life!"

- Frank Kitchen and Rodger Campbell

In 2009, I ran in and completed my very first marathon, The Phoenix Rock and Roll Marathon. While running the ungodly distance of 26.2 miles, many thoughts went through my head:

"Why am I doing this?"

"Where is the finish line?"

"Where is my wife?"

"Where is the finish line?"

"That guy is running barefoot!"

"Where is the finish line?"

I also noticed that I was running the race with 10,000 *BAD APPLES*..

What does *BAD APPLE* mean? When I travel the country with my speaking partner, Rodger Campbell, we are always asked that very question. We both believe that people and organizations are like apples. They have the ability to grow into something ordinary or extraordinary, or to simply rot.

Our goal is for everyone to become extraordinary. In order to do this you must become B.A.D. Don't worry; being B.A.D. in this case is a good thing. B.A.D. means to have belief, action and determination.

Belief:

We all have dreams in our lives, but do we really believe they can come true? My dream was to run and complete a marathon. One marathon. In order for my dream to become reality, I needed to believe that I could complete the race. Without belief, there is no action. A dream that doesn't come true becomes a nightmare. Taking the first step to achieve a dream is the toughest part. You can only take that leap of faith when you truly believe.

Action:

Now that I believed, I needed to take action. My actions included six months of training, consulting with running experts, buying the right equipment, and putting down my non-refundable entry fee. As the race date got closer, I started having doubts. I considered changing my mind, right until my last practice run. I ran over twenty miles with my wife and I didn't die! My marathon dream could really happen. I was about to accomplish something extraordinary

Determination:

Race day arrived with the harsh 4 a.m. sound of my alarm clock beep beep beep-ing. I got up and got ready. I ate my carbs, drank my fluids, and took ibuprofen. Excitement filled my body as the race began. My excitement faded around mile 13. That is when things really got tough. At mile 18, I thought about quitting when my right leg cramped up. It was agonizing. The thought of not accomplishing my dream kept me going. I really didn't want to have to run the race again. I mentally stayed determined. When other muscles started to lock up, I found the first aid station to get treatment. When I thought that I was the only one having issues, I looked around and saw hundreds of other people facing similar difficulties. Our torment bonded us. As the finish line approached, I saw my friends cheering for me. Brian, Teresa, Chad, Tracy, Caden, and Cole gave me the final push needed to cross the finish line.

When I crossed the line, my celebration and marathon retirement began. With bags of ice on my knees and ibuprofen in my mouth, I waited for my wife to cross the finish line. Her smile was part relief and part exhilaration. The smile on her face was similar to the thousands runners who finished the race. It was the smile of accomplishment. Completing the race was the achievement of a dream.

No matter what you want to accomplish, you must be B.A.D. First, you must *believe* in the dream. Second, you have to take the proper *action*. Finally, when the hardships arise you must stay *determined* to the end. Hardships will definitely test your beliefs, but if you stay determined, you can accomplish your dreams.

When you accomplish your dreams, it's more than ordinary...it's special. Feel the pride of your accomplishment and you can't wait to conquer your next challenge. This is success. This is what it means to be a is being a BAD APPLE.

For more information on The BAD, BAD APPLES, go to: www.badbadapples.com

CHAPTER 18

THE GOOD LUCK SEVEN

"We make a living by what we get, but we make a life by what we give."

— Winston Churchill

Speaking to and mentoring youth is an amazing experience. My wife and her   co-workers invited me to speak to a group of 8th graders at their school in Phoenix, Arizona. It was the last day of school, and they wanted someone to entertain and educate the students. It was a half -day for the students and teachers. No one knew how many kids to expect

Over one hundred and seventy-five kids showed up for the last day of classes and my program. I remembered when I was a kid in school and guest speakers came to lecture us. I didn't want that to be me. In the dictionary, the definition of lecture is not positive. I wanted the kids to have a positive experience. I had two hours and thirty minutes to impact the lives of kids that I'd never met. It turned into two hours and thirty minutes of fun.

The program was held in the school library. It didn't look like much of a library after we were done. My favorite moment of that day happened about an hour after the program. I was sitting in a diner near the school with my wife and her co-workers. We were talking about the program. Several students noticed me and came over to thank me. That made me feel good, but something made me feel better: it came from the student who didn't talk to me. A young girl was sitting in a booth with her mother. You could see they were talking about her day. During the conversation,

I noticed the girl pull out my handouts and explain them to her mother.

At that point, I was basking at how great I was, but to see the real impact of my presentation suddenly made me feel humble and grateful to have impacted this young girl's life. I may not have impacted the lives of every child in that library, but I was able to impact at least one.

The program was called "Good Luck in High School." It was over two hours of games, activities and a small bit of lecturing on what will make the students successful in High School, and in life. I mixed in a few prizes to help out. At the end of the program, I handed out cards containing my *Good Luck 7*. Seven is a lucky number, so the students and I participated in seven activities they could use to prepare themselves to be lucky in life.

When preparation meets opportunity, you get lucky. Here are the seven lucky tips I shared with the students to assist them achieve success in life.

1. Success comes from work.
2. Have the proper attitude.
3. A.S.K. Questions (Always Seek Knowledge).
4. Develop your own identity.
5. Make strong and healthy relationships.
6. Help others.
7. Learn new stuff.

CHAPTER 19

HOW NEGATIVE ARE YOU?

"Life can be one big traffic jam. You can stay stuck on the highway of life or you can find a way around the traffic."
— Frank Kitchen

Why is it that every time you have to be somewhere at a specific time, you seem to run into traffic? There are unexpected car accidents, slow drivers, and household appliances in the middle of the road; there is unnecessary construction and there are roadblocks. I've learned that a negative attitude, doing negative things, or making negative comments are all mental roadblocks.

When a roadblock appears, detours must be found. Questions must be asked: "what now?" "what can I do?" and "what are the possibilities?" Navigating around any roadblock takes action. Mostly, it's hard work. It's easier to stay in one spot and complain, but complaining and being negative gets you nowhere. That is what most people do, isn't it? They simply stay in one place and don't advance. Isn't that more frustrating than the hard work of navigating around the roadblock?

Last Lecture author Randy Pausch said that "barriers are put into our lives for the purpose of showing how badly we want something." Negativity is a huge barrier for a lot of people. It's easy to be negative. When someone asks, "tell me something good about yourself," it takes time, it requires thought. But if you're asked to think about the negative, the answers come easy. Why is that? People invariably say, "that's just the way it is!" But I ask, "does it have to be that way?" and "what can be done to change the situation?" Positive people will come up with a list of options and plans to improve things. Negative people will complain about reasons things can't work.

Two things can happen: the negative people can bring the positive people down, or the positive people can help change the attitudes of the negative people. Ultimately, it's up to the negative people to look at themselves in the mirror and mentally challenge themselves to change their attitudes and beliefs. It will take work, but eventually they will discover, that in the long run it's easier to be positive than it is to give up when they encounter a roadblock. Being negative is the roadblock to people advancing in life.

CHAPTER 20

THE FLOATING SANDAL

"Everyday we have over 10,000 interactions! We need 5 positive interactions to negate every negative interaction."
— *How Full is your Bucket, 2004*

Every day, we have the opportunity to make a choice. You can choose to do something positive or negative. The choice can affect the life of someone else in a positive or negative way. If a rotten apple can spoil the bunch, what happens with a positive apple?

Many of my experiences at the Phoenix Zoo are worth sharing. My adventure with the "floating sandal" is one that made me feel really good inside.

My shift had just ended. It was a long walk to the time clock. I was walking with my co-worker, Kelly. We talked about the long and tiring day. We couldn't wait to get home. As we passed the elephant exhibit, we noticed a child limping. The little girl was with her parents and younger brother. I looked at her feet and noticed that she was missing a sandal. I asked her, "what happened to your sandal?" In tears she responded, "it's in the lake." The girl's parents told us that the sandal was in the lake near the children's trail and would be impossible to get.

Seeing the little girl in tears, we felt it was worth an attempt to find the sandal. The girl wouldn't stop crying. We pulled out our radios and called for an available zookeeper. We would need a boat to retrieve the sandal. Kelly had a very important event to get to, so I told her I would assist the family. The family followed me to the trail. I asked the girl how her sandal got in the lake. I really couldn't decipher what she was saying between the crying, sniffling, and deep breaths. Her brother said, "the sandal is floating in the lake near the monkeys."

This sounded easy. Just find the sandal floating near the monkeys. All we would need is a boat from a keeper and something to scoop it up. We arrived at the bridge near the monkeys. The boy yelled out: "there it is!"

The sandal was there. It was floating in the green algae on the opposite side of the monkey's lake. Every zoo employee knew this area was full of cattails and mud deep enough to swallow anyone whole.

The good news was that the sandal was floating a mere ten feet from the shore. The bad news was that it was about ten feet from the shore. Tangled palm fronds and floating debris would make this a tough catch. The parents told me not to worry about it, but I really thought that I could get it. That's when one of the keepers, Cat, arrived. I explained to her what was happening and asked for a long rake. As she handed it to me, she reminded me to be careful.

With my rake in hand, I headed down to the shoreline to fish out the sandal. It was a more of an embankment, a very wet embankment with terrible footing. What I thought was solid ground was actually floating debris. My left foot slid into the water and got more than a little wet. This is when the Cat told me, "don't fall in the water!"

The rake wasn't long enough, but I couldn't give up. Again, the parents told us not to worry about it and that we had done enough. That's when we noticed a long palm branch near the shore. It was just the right length to reach the sandal.

From a safe and dry spot, I was able to use the end of the branch to drag the sandal closer to shore. When it got closer, I used the rake to fish out the sandal. Victoriously I cried out that I found the sandal. I turned to see the little girl and her mother displaying big smiles. I returned the sandal to its proper owner. Cat pointed the family to the nearest restroom and recommended they wash the sandal off. The parents thanked us for all of our help and walked toward the restroom.

With one soggy shoe and one dry shoe, I arrived to the time clock. My manager asked about my radio calls. I explained the details of my mission to return Cinderella's slipper. My manager told me, "Nice job, you didn't have to do that."

When I first stared working at the zoo, I was told we needed to do wild things to make our guests happy. The sandal may not be important to a lot of people, but it was important to the little girl. She wasn't happy on her way out the first time, but by the time we got her sandal out of the water, she and her family were happy. The experience made me feel really good inside as I drove home. I know that positive experience made the family feel good about the Phoenix Zoo and the people who work there.

CHAPTER 21

MY ROLE MODEL: FRANKIE KITCHEN

"We learn 80% of what we need by the age of four years old, the rest of our life is spent perfecting what we learned."

- Edith Mack Gordon

Do you remember when you were a child? Do you remember your lack of fear? Do you remember the constant energy that you had? Were you on a constant quest to find out how things work? Can you believe the hairstyles and clothes your parents forced on you? Do you ever wish you could go back and do it all over again?

When I was growing up, everyone knew me as Frankie. My dad was Frank, so I was called Frankie. There is a picture of Frankie on the back cover of this book. He's on there because he is one of my role models. Frankie was a cool kid. His afro was remarkable. His smile lit up a room. His questions were constant. He was an explorer. He had a solution for every problem. He loved to play sports. He was inventive. He got along with everyone. He was a dreamer.

One of Frankie's dreams was to be older, so everyone would stop treating him like a child. He told everyone to call him Frank when he turned 13. At 13, he was no longer a child. He was a teenager. "Teenagers don't have kid nicknames" was his proclamation. He didn't want to be treated like a child anymore. No more sitting at the kid's table for family holidays. No baby sitters. No bedtime. This was laughable considering he still played with his Voltron and GI Joe toys. He still went Trick or Treating, had no facial hair on his face, was shorter than all of the girls in school, and spent time at home making the world's best lemon cakes in his sister's Easy Bake Oven.

I miss Frankie. As I've aged, I've become Frank to everyone. A few people still call me Frankie, mostly family and friends who have known me for a long time. Every time I hear that name, a smile comes to my face. I spent my childhood wanting to be an adult; now, I spend my adult years wishing I could be that little kid again.

As we grow older, society tells us to stop acting like a child. We are told be serious, and to grow up. We grow up and forget about what makes life fun and interesting. Getting older doesn't mean we can't have fun in our lives. Instead of thinking why or why not, adults start thinking no or that's not possible.

Children should be our role models. They are sponges. They learn anything and everything at an amazing rate. To a child, everything is possible. Discovery is a fun challenge. There's always a back door or another way. They enjoy the challenge of getting things done. The simplest things can be turned into something fun and exciting. That's how I like it.

I would love to be five years old again - minus the afro and polyester suit. I would love to have the passion and spirit to appreciate the little things. I want to explore the world, laugh all the time, spend time with friends, do things I enjoy and not worry about what other people think; I want to enjoy life.

CHAPTER 22

FCK?

~

"It takes more courage to reveal insecurities than to hide them."
- Alex Karras

The letters FCK make up my initials. My name is Frank Cornelius Kitchen. Yes, I am named after a room in a house. My name has provided me with a lifetime of teasing, questions, and strength.

People have asked, "do you cook franks in the kitchen?" I've been referred to as living room, dining room, bathroom, and bedroom. It took me years to learn how to spell my middle name. When I got older, I learned my initials are not the best initials when initialing important documents. I tell everyone that it could have been worse. My parents could have named me Frank Ulysses Kitchen. I'll give you time to figure out those initials.

My name could have caused a lot of mental scars, but my name has given me strength. I often tell audiences how my mom loved monogramming everything she purchased for me as a child. I had interesting discussions with my high school teachers when I showed up to school wearing a monogrammed turtleneck. It was monogrammed with the letters FCK.

There are people who consider my name a joke. For me, the joke has turned into a source of pride and strength. I am named after my father and grandfather. My first name is my father's name and my middle name is my grandfather's name. Both have served the United States in the armed forces. They have protected the freedoms that I enjoy today. They have provided me the freedom to write this book. I also have one of the most memorable last names. No one ever forgets the guy named *Kitchen.*

My initials are interesting. I was taught that you need a *hook* when it comes to marketing yourself. My initials are that hook. I've made t-shirts using them. How amazing is it to have the pastor of your church ask for a t-shirt that reads *FCK* on the front and *All I need is U* on the back? I tell people around the world that, "I provide *Fresh* and *Creative Knowledge* that educates, inspires and entertains; to do this all I need is *You* and an opportunity to shine." There are so many options:

Fun, Caring and Kind
Fun, Cool, Kid
Fundamentals, Create Know-how
Get F.C.K.'d (Get Fresh and Creative Knowledge Daily)

Life should be enjoyed. You should have fun. No one is perfect. You possess unique abilities and talents. They can hold you back or give you strength. The choice is yours.

CHAPTER 23

ARE YOU LOOKING OUT FOR NUMBER ONE?

"Busy means something else is more important."

— Frank Kitchen

A re you looking out for number one? It is an important, thought-provoking question. The question popped into my head one night when I finally did something to take care of myself. I was getting a massage through massage therapy program at Lakeland Community College. The program looks for volunteers their students can work on. The massages were relaxing. They work out the kinks in muscles that I didn't know existed.

While I was lying face down on the table, I started thinking about how an hour of *me time* would help out in several areas of my life. The thoughts came from a handout one of my good friends had shared with me. It listed things people could do to live more productive and healthy lives. There were comments about healthy eating, finances, and natural living. I was drawn to two bullet points.

- Dedicate at least one hour to yourself daily.
- Stress is linked to the six leading causes of death: heart disease, cancer, lung ailments, accidents, liver cirrhosis, and suicide.

My friend told me that he rarely does anything to take care of himself. He put a lot of his time and energy into work and other endeavors. He was stressed, run down, and unmotivated. He said: "I really need to take care of myself, I don't have the energy to spend time with my wife and kids." His family was his number one priority, but he wasn't living that way.

We started to talk, and I asked him what he did for himself. This is a question that I've asked a lot of people: do you look out for number one?

I heard a health expert Deanna Latson make a great comment: "People spend more time taking care of their homes, cars, material items, and work than themselves. You can get a new job and new possessions, but you only get one body!"

That really made me think. You can't have healthy relationships, possessions, or work, if you don't take care yourself. If you're not healthy mentally or physically you won't be able to take care of yourself or the people you care about. If you're not alive, you can't have possessions, let alone a job.

Your life is the most important thing that you posses. Many fail to think this way. People put more time and effort into work than themselves. They hoard vacation time while making comments like, "I can't take a vacation because I'll have a ton of work to do when I get back." People don't look out for their number one. You must remove stress and negatives from your life. De-stress before your unpleasant mood and actions poorly affect the relationships you have with the people closest to you. If you don't rest, you perform poorly at work and other activities that are important to you. If you don't watch your health, you can't be there for your spouse, significant other, family, or friends. It all comes back to taking proper care of your body and yourself.

Isn't it amazing how people will treat cars better than themselves? People will get service on their car, but won't take time to go in for a check-up at the doctor. They'll get their car washed and detailed, but won't take care of their body.

I hope that reading this will encourage you to take time to figure what you can do for yourself to make yourself happier, stress-free, healthier, motivated, and positive. You can't do anything for others if you're not around. Once you take care of yourself, you'll have a better chance to achieving all of your hopes and dreams. For people who say they are too busy or don't have time, think about following:

People make time to watch their favorite television shows, but can't make time to exercise.

People get premium gasoline for their cars, but buy second-rate food to put in their stomachs.

People constantly say that they are too busy, then complain that they can't do the things that are important to them.

Busy means something else is more important at the time. If something is truly important, you will make time for it. Life is short, do what you can to enjoy it, and live it to the best of your abilities. Take care of yourself and take care of the one thing you'll only get one of... you!

CHAPTER 24

VACATION TIME

~~~

"I need a vacation" – countless people worldwide

Have you caught yourself saying the line above over and over again? I have. Anytime I catch myself saying those words, I go on a vacation. You can too. You're probably saying, "I can't afford to go on a vacation." Or, you might be saying, "I don't have the time to take a vacation." You're also thinking, "Frank must have a lot of money." The answers are simple. Yes, you can afford a vacation. Yes, you have the time to take a vacation. You don't need a lot of money, but you need to know the meaning of the word vacation.

Vacation is defined as a period of recreation. Recreation is defined as an activity done for enjoyment when one is not working. Simply put, a vacation is a time for you to enjoy yourself by not working. What are some of the things you can do to enjoy life?

Life is a wonderful thing. It is something to enjoy. You can spend it all working. You need time to recharge your battery. You need time to turn your brain off and enjoy yourself. This is why people flock to comedy films at the movie theater. Critics will give poor reviews to *silly* and *childish* movies. The very same movies will be the most popular movie of the year. Why is that? People need recreation. People need time to de-stress their bodies and minds.

The human body is an amazing machine. As with any machine, it can be overworked, over used and over stressed. You can give it brief or extended periods of time off. Some people think extended time off is the only way – this is not true. A brief break can do wonders for your body.

I asked what you do to enjoy life. Did you write them down? I am sure that there are activities on your list that cost money. I am betting that there a few that don't cost money. This means that you can afford to take a vacation. Any period of time can be a vacation. People have just been programmed to think a vacation has to last several days. People believe you can only call it a vacation when you leave town. Time in the park reading a book can be classified as a vacation. It's recreation. It's time from work. It's something you can do to enjoy life.

This is where you say, "I don't have time to read a book." You also say, "I don't have time to take a vacation." Wrong and wrong! First, you're reading this book. Thank you! Second, you make time for what you want. Stop using the excuse, "I'm too busy." Busy means something else is more important. Anything you find important you have to make time for. Just like a long vacation, you need to write *short vacation* times on your calendar. When you write vacation on your calendar, everything gets put on hold. Your vacation is important and you have made time for it. Give yourself a daily vacation. Even if it's only for a few minutes, it will be good for you and your health.

Going on a vacation puts you in a positive mental state. The moment you begin your vacation, everything about you is positive. You smile more. Your body language is out of this world. Your confidence is sky high. You are relaxed and ready to enjoy yourself. Wouldn't that mindset and feeling be great to have all the time? You can have it – just by changing your mindset.

You have to recognize that you need to take time to enjoy yourself, no matter how short or long the period of time. You must realize that this is the true definition of a vacation. You need to acknowledge that you don't need a lot of money to take a vacation. There are countless forms of recreational activities you can do that cost little or no money. Finally, you have to establish set times for you to vacation. Once you put something on your calendar, your mindset changes. Vacations are important to you. Once you're on vacation, it's the only thing you are thinking about. You're not thinking about work. You're not thinking about the stresses of your life. You're just enjoying yourself.

Happy vacationing. Feel free to send me pictures of you on your vacation. It will make your vacation feel more real and I'll be excited to see you enjoying yourself.

CHAPTER 25

THE ELEPHANT DOESN'T LIKE ME?

"The story you are about to read is true. Only the names have been changed to protect the innocent."

— 1950s Television show, Dragnet

Not everyone is going to like you in life. It's the truth. Someone may not like the way you look another person may not like how you act. Others may not like the way you do things. A few may not like you because they are jealous of your abilities. It is their prerogative, but do they respect you?

I was working at the *African Wildlife Park* performing the *Animal Adventure* talk. I was talking to a large crowd about our African elephants. I was giving fun facts and stories about our family of five. During the talks, I handed out carrots to the crowd. They threw the carrots into the exhibit to help feed the elephants. It was a great experience for the little kids and the big kids. When I say big kids, I mean the adults.

I always told the crowds to respect the elephants by not throwing the carrots in their pond, hitting the elephants with the carrots, or yelling at them.

During the talk, the elephant named Peanut started to walk away. I wanted him to come closer to the crowd. I tossed a couple of carrots in front of him in hopes he would come over to eat them. That didn't work, so I tried talking to him. I said, "come here Peanut, the people want to see you." Then, I made a large swinging motion with my right arm, the motion you would make when you're trying to get someone to come towards you. He came over and waved his trunk up and down; he didn't look happy. That was very unusual for Peanut, so I spoke to some co-workers after the talk. I asked if I had done something wrong. I asked if I had upset the elephant.

Word quickly spread around the wildlife park that I had upset Peanut. Co-workers were teasing me that I had pissed off the elephants. They joked about what other animals at the park I could upset. I asked, "does Peanut hate me?"

I was worried, so my friend Penny talked to the elephant keepers. She told me, "the elephant doesn't like you." What did that mean? The elephant didn't like me? Did he not like my voice? Did he not like other men? Did he not like the color of my skin? Was the elephant racist? Was I going to loose my job for upsetting the elephant?

Seeing the look on my face, Penny smiled and told me she was joking. She told me that my hand gesture could have signaled Peanut to raise his trunk. He had been a part of a circus before coming to the wildlife park. His former trainers may have taught him the trunk motion. I was relieved, but still had months of jokes to endure. I did play a few jokes on my own. I told my one co-worker that I couldn't work around the elephants because they didn't like me. Pete listened to the full story as I explained my fears. Being a concerned individual, Pete told me he was going to get some answers. That's when I told him the truth. He laughed.

I talked to the keepers and asked what I should and shouldn't do around the elephants. They explained that animals are just like people. They have personalities. They have good days and not so good days. Peanut wasn't in the mood for carrots that day. There have been no issues with the elephants since that day. We are still putting smiles on children's faces daily.

Life isn't about having someone or something like you. Life is about earning the respect of an individual or group. No one wants to be disliked. I spent days trying to find out if an elephant didn't like me. I should have

done more to learn more about the elephants. You earn respect
practice what you preach and live up to your promises. You earn respe.
from others when you take the time to learn about them. You learn their
personalities. You discover their likes and dislikes. You take the time to
truly understand the motivations and passions. People spend too much
time trying to motivate others to like them. It is nice to be liked, but it's
better to be respected.

CHAPTER 26

IS THERE AN AWARD FOR SHARING YOUR WISDOM?

~~~~~~~

"It's one thing to go out and buy a gift, the gift becomes special when you make it yourself."

– Frank Kitchen

When I worked at Lakeland Community College, I had the opportunity to work with some phenomenal students. They truly impacted my life in positive ways. This chapter is about one of those phenomenal students.

One Spring day, I walked into my office and found a nice surprise waiting for me. There was a handmade Yoda statue on my desk. It had the following inscription on the bottom:

To Frank:

Thanks for all you do. Great Friend, you are.

May the Force be with you!

Amelia

It was made by one of the students who worked for me. She is a huge Star Wars fan. She gave me the Yoda for assisting her transfer to another school. My students and co-workers knew that I was a *Star Wars* fan too. A few called me Yoda. They often teased me by saying, "You share your wisdom, but you can be hard to understand!"

Amelia was off to film school, but found the time to make a gift and bring it to my office. She told me that my "Yoda Award" was a sign of appreciation for all the help I gave. I told Amelia that I expected to see her name on the big screen someday. Truth be told, I am confident that she will win an Oscar some day. When I see her win her award, I'll be sure to look at my "Yoda Award" and smile.

There were days that I wondered why I did my job at the college. Then, special days like that one occurred. Never forget to share your wisdom, knowledge, and experiences with the people around you. You may not receive a physical award, but you will be rewarded. You have the ability to make the world a better place. By sharing, you affect your life and the lives of others.

I recently re-connected with Amelia via Facebook. She is living in Hollywood and working in the film industry. I let her know that I still have my award and how special it is to me. She wrote back. Here's what she wrote:

Thank you for embracing Yoda all these years. That really meant a lot to me to know that he is traveling the country with you.

Please let me know when you will be in town. And also, let me know how that book is coming along. You inspired many of us back in Ohio.

Amelia

CHAPTER 27

FRANKISMS

~~~

"Frankism: A statement, piece of advice or analogy given by Frank Kitchen. Frankisms are shared with friends, family members, and people to provide inspiration or motivation."

– Teresa Whittaker

Teresa Whittaker is a sister to me. She is a master of observation, brutally honest, and she is someone that I seek out for advice. Her family and friends rely on her for support in good time and not so good times.

I am often the brunt of Teresa's jokes. She likes to tease me on a variety of things I do or say. She likes to call me her big brother and she treats me that way. One day, I posted some words of wisdom on Facebook. The first person to respond was Teresa. Her response, "thanks for that Frankism." Teresa had just created a new word for the world. She was making fun of me, but I wasn't upset. The new word was perfect. *Frankism:* .

I love reading and collecting quotes. Reading these words, statements, and thoughts have inspired me pursue and achieve many of my dreams. Some have caused me to dream more. Most give me that *Woo Hoo* feeling inside.

My goal in life is simple. I would like to *Educate, Inspire and Entertain* people with fresh and creative knowledge. I typically do this by sharing my thoughts and ideas. They are called *Frankisms*. Here a few of my favorites:

- "Remember the past, appreciate the present and work to make the future happen!"
- "You can't go somewhere physically or fiscally until you go there mentally first!"
- "Life is about relationships and experiences! Enjoy them and make the most out of them!"
- "It's more fun when there's more than one."
- "Tomorrow starts today."
- "Choose people to work with, not work for."
- "Life is like a puzzle! You just have to put the pieces together the right way to see your vision!"
- "Believe in yourself or no one else will!"
- "Be a doer not at knower! Knowing something doesn't mean you can do something!"
- "You have to really want to do something before you can go after it and accomplish it!"
- "Being a leader is like using a credit card. Many of us don't learn how to do it right until we max ourselves out!"
- "Life is about attitude! The right attitude will take you far! The wrong attitude will take you nowhere! Which attitude will you choose?"
- "The higher your expectations are, the higher your level of desire, effort, knowledge and skill must be to turn your expectations into reality!"
- "The more you want something, the harder you have to work to obtain it!"
- "Hard work will take you far, but working smarter will take you farther!"
- "Good friends and family make a difference."

- "Everyone you meet in your life has value and the ability to impact your life! Treat them that way and amazing things will happen!"
- "Life is about what you can do, not what you can't!"
- "How much love are you giving your dream?"
- 'Life is about challenges! The key is if you will accept the challenge to push yourself!"
- "It is better to be respected than liked, but if you can be liked and respected watch out!"
- "Make life about *how it should be* and not about *how it is*."
- "I may not be the smartest person in the world, but I do have eyes."
- "Live Life!"
- "Do you want hit your goals or exceed them? Be the best you, you can be. Don't settle for anything less."
- "Don't wait for your dreams to happen, make them happen! Wait = Wishing An Idea Turnsout."
- "Do you follow the advice you give to others?"
- "When you practice what you preach good things will happen for you. When you preach but don't practice, watch out."
- "To be a true role model, you have to model the actions you want to see out of others."

Now it's time for you to make your very own –ism. You are an amazing person. You have the ability to impact your life and the lives of the people around you. Sharing your wisdom, thoughts, and ideas is just one way to do this. Please take the time on a piece of paper to write down some of your favorite quotes and thoughts.

I'd love to read your quotes. Please send them to me. You can send them to me via e-mail, Twitter or Facebook. You'll find all of the information at the end of this book.

CHAPTER 28

DO YOU HAVE A SUPER HERO COSTUME?

"Who has confidence in himself will gain the confidence of others."

— Lieb Lazarow

You are a Super Hero! It may have be hard to believe, but it's true. You are a super hero because you possess abilities and talents that people may be jealous of. You are unique. You are special. Your abilities and talents can be used for good. You help people around the world. The only question is, "do you have a super hero costume?"

Every Super Hero has a costume. They come from different parts of the globe, from different planets; some come from different dimensions. Super Heroes have a variety of super powers that others don't have. They have different beliefs and purposes. Some Super Heroes are simply different. The one thing they do have in common is a costume. They have a costume or costumes that gives them confidence. The costumes give them confidence to display their abilities.

Many people lack the confidence to showcase their talents and abilities. Many times, this lack of confidence is based on appearance. Have you ever lacked confidence because you didn't like the way you looked? Has anyone ever told you to be comfortable in your own skin?

A Super Hero's confidence comes from their costume. I am sure that you can think of several Super Heroes that do *super* things once they're in a costume. As their alter ego, they cannot do much. They lack confidence. In their costume, anything is possible. That brings me to you.

Do you have clothing that makes you feel powerful? Do you have a power suit? You know, that suit you wear when you go for that big interview. I was not a big fan of fashion growing up. A t-shirt and jeans were just fine for me. As I got older, my Mom constantly bothered me about making a great first impression. She told me that I needed to watch how I dress. She was right; I needed to dress more professionally. I would be treated like a child if I dressed like one. I wanted to be a part of the professional world, so I really needed to look the part.

I hated getting dressed up. Everything felt uncomfortable. The more uncomfortable I felt, the less confidence I had. I needed help. Franco and Dominic Terriaco were my saviors. The brothers run *Terriaco Suit and Tailoring* in Mentor, Ohio. They treated me like family. They educated me on how to dress. I was taught about quality. I was shown how clothing should properly fit. They showed me what clothes worked best for me. It's amazing how much confidence you gain when you look at yourself in the mirror and feel good about what you are wearing.

In order for you to accomplish your dreams, you need confidence. Call it confidence or superstition, there are endless stories about people wearing a favorite article of clothing to give them confidence. Athletes wear special socks. A woman may wear her favorite shoes. Businessmen wear power ties. Actors wear their favorite color. Bruce Wayne becomes *Batman* by putting on a mask and suit. These are all examples of clothing making the man or woman.

Look in your closet: what clothing makes you feel good about yourself? What gives you confidence? These items are your super hero costumes. They give you confidence, strength, and the ability to take on the world. You must have the proper mindset to pursue your dreams. My fashion education made me feel like I could take on the world. Anytime I went into a meeting or an interview my attire gave me confidence. To this day, Franco and Dominic are still advising me on what I should and shouldn't wear.

When you need assistance putting together the perfect wardrobe, contact the brothers. They will show you how to dress with confidence for any occasion or event. They teach you how to create a style that matches your personality with your body type. Tell them that Frankie sent you.

Terriaco Suits & Tailoring

8837 Mentor Ave, Mentor, Ohio

440-974-9119

CHAPTER 29

DO IT MENTALLY BEFORE YOU DO IT PHYSICALLY

"Dress for the job you want, not the job you have!"

— Unknown

I really like the quote above. My best friend Scott shared it with me while we were on vacation. The quote came up while we were sitting by the pool at a Las Vegas hotel. We were talking about people pursuing their dreams. We were discussing why people succeed or fail in achieving their dreams.

I believe the quote is all about an individual's mindset. Everyone has dreams, but what are you doing mentally to achieve your dreams? Before you can physically do something, you have to imagine it. You have to completely believe that you can do it mentally.

I read an article about actor Matthew McConaughey that weekend. He was quoted several times in the article. One particular quote opened my eyes. He said, "you have to tie your shoes first." He was talking about running. Simply put, he was saying that you have to prepare mentally for the activity you are going to do *before* you do it.

Many people think they can turn a switch and change overnight. Here are a few examples.

A smoker talks about how he wants to quit smoking. In order to dress the part, he needs to start cutting back on his smoking. He has to start mentally acting like a non-smoker.

You constantly read about people going on fad diets or having surgery to help them lose weight. Months later, the weight is back on. Mentally, they never changed their eating habits. They didn't commit to a healthy lifestyle or exercise routine.

Finally, you hear people talk about taking care of their finances. They talk about what they're going to do when they get out of debt. Talk is great, but what are they doing now? Are they saving their money or making smart purchases? Are they reading books to educate themselves about financial affairs? Don't be like these people: prepare yourself before you get there. Many times, it starts with asking questions.

CHAPTER 30

THE POWER OF ASKING QUESTIONS

"One who asks a question is a fool for five minutes; one who does not ask a question remains a fool forever."

— *Chinese Proverb*

It was my college graduation day. After twelve years of hard work, I was finally walking across the stage to receive my college degree. I wanted to share the moment with the people closest to me, my family. Strangely, not seeing them in the crowd made me feel alone. As I waited for the ceremony to begin, I heard a cheer from the crowd, "hey, Frank!" My brother, sister, and mother were there to support me. My loneliness suddenly left me. The rest of the ceremony was a happy blur. I barely remember getting my diploma. After the ceremony, I was anxious to see my family at the graduate reception. Hugs were exchanged and photos were taken. I noticed my mother had a nervous look on her face after the photos. I asked her if something was wrong. She responded, "there she is!"

I looked over my shoulder to see our commencement speaker, the late Congresswoman Stephanie Tubbs Jones. My mother had seen her deliver a speech at the 2004 Democratic National Convention and was a huge fan. I told my mom to ask her for a photograph. She told me, "I'm too scared to ask. What if she says no?" My mother, the woman I knew as fearless, was lacking the courage to approach someone that she idolized. That's when I told her, "it never hurts to ask... if you don't do it, I will!" "No, I'll do it," she responded. My pep talk had given her the needed push to introduce herself to the Congresswoman. My mother told her how she admired her and would like a photograph with her. Congresswoman Jones not only obliged, but cheerfully invited all of us over for a group photo.

Soon, everyone noticed the Congresswoman was in the room and approached for their opportunity to take a photo with her. Her assistant informed the gathering crowd that the Congresswoman had another appointment and needed to leave. The last photo she took that day was with my mother. The courage to approach the Congresswoman and ask a simple question created a special moment that we wouldn't forget. Several people approached my mother and made the same comment, "I wish I had the courage to ask for a photograph!" That courage made me proud of my mother.

My mother didn't realize it, but she was a leader. She was motivating herself toward her goal of talking to an idol and inspiring her children. Leaders are people of action. Leaders have a drive and passion that unites the people they lead. Throughout our young lives, my mother taught my brother, sister, and I to work hard towards accomplishing our dreams. It is one thing to speak wisdom, but it is something completely different to *demonstrate wisdom*. Her dream of meeting her idol inspired her children. She showed us that it takes action to accomplish a dream. Her fear did not prevent her from achieving her dream.

My mother's courage was fueled by asking questions. She asked me for my input. Then she asked the congresswoman a question. The ability to gain strength and courage comes from our ability to ask questions. A.S.K. means to always seek knowledge: always seek knowledge! That's what I preach with my good friend Rodger Campbell. Leaders ask questions. Successful leaders accomplish their dreams faster, smarter, and with less mistakes when they take the time to ask questions.

People make mistakes, but the point is not to repeat mistakes. By asking questions, people can avoid mistakes and pitfalls. People fear asking questions for a variety of reasons. The key to asking questions is working up the courage to ask. It is important to realize that asking questions can only get you closer to your dreams. You never lose ground when asking questions. You can stay in the same place or advance forward. You can advance forward by asking these three questions.

1. What do I want?

2. What is its value to me?

3. How do I get it?

Dreams are what we want. I always suggest that individuals or organizations write down all of their dreams on a piece of paper. Did you write your "Grocery List" earlier in this book (in Chapter 9)? When you were writing or drawing your list, did you dream the big dream? If you didn't, here is your second chance to write down everything you ever dreamed of doing on piece of paper. Don't limit yourself. Write down needs and wants. After you've completed the list, look at it. Now ask yourself, "what do I really value?" You can also ask, "why is it valuable and important to me?" Finally, you need to ask the final question, "what do I do to make my dreams come true?" The answer is simple. Ask questions. There are no stupid questions. However, it is possible to ask the wrong questions or worse, not asking questions at all.

The most important question you can ask is, "do I need help?" The courage to admit that you need help is very important. Recognize that you cannot do everything yourself. Surround yourself with good people and listen to their ideas. Successful people surround themselves with people they trust and can turn to for advice; these are people who aren't afraid to tell you that you are heading down the wrong path, or to tell you that there is something that you may have overlooked something that will assist in making the dream become reality. Asking for help is the ability to delegate. It is the ability to value the dream coming true versus thinking you are better than everyone else.

No matter how new or fresh the dream, someone has been there before or had a similar experience. There are people who have been successful at accomplishing dreams similar to yours. These people aren't any better than you. They are just a little further down the trail of success. Research and learn about these people. Find them, contact them, and communicate with them. When you meet these people, take time to ask questions. Be sure to explain your dream. Then, ask questions to discover the obstacles that may deter you from accomplishing your dreams. Questions help you achieve your dreams. The courage to ask questions comes from the belief that you have in the dream. Without belief, there is no reality.

CHAPTER 31

THE LITTLE THINGS TO LEADERSHIP

What is leadership? Leadership isn't easy. It requires time, energy, and both physical and fiscal investments. Much is known about leadership, but there is no one definition for leadership. Author Joe Roest found 221 different definitions of leadership while writing his book *Leadership in the 21st Century.*

Forbes Magazine reported that over $15 billion is spent annually in the United States teaching executives about leadership. That's over 14.5 tons in twenty-dollar bills spent every year just to train the hierarchy of organizations. That doesn't cover students, employees, and supervisors.

Leadership is important. I believe *leadership* is the ability to inspire, motivate, or encourage an individual or group to accomplish a dream. We all want to be successful leaders, and we want to work with successful leaders. The dilemma with leadership is that we focus so much on the goal or outcome that we forget about the little things.

> *"Enjoy the little things in life for one day you'll look back and realize they were the big things."*
>
> *– Kurt Vonnegut*

Luck is when preparation meets opportunity. Being a successful leader requires luck. The ultimate lucky number is *seven*. Here are *Seven Little Things* that you can do to become a highly effective leader.

1. Show Genuine Interest.

Study the people you lead. Know their strengths and their opportunities for growth; know their likes and dislikes, know their motivations. Don't treat the people you lead like a number. Know each of them as an individual.

2. Be Visible.

Be a role model. Set the example. Show up for the activities you ask others to attend. Let people see you working. Actively display the behaviors you want people to exhibit.

3. Be a Teacher.

Provide people with a vision and teach people how to make that vision come true. Invest the time and resources to train people thoroughly and constantly. Develop a training program that helps people grow.

4. Delegate.

You can't do everything yourself. Discover the talents of the people you lead. Use their talents to accomplish the goal or vision. Put people in positions to excel and grow.

5. Do the S-ugar H-oney I-ce T-ea Jobs!

Don't delegate only dirty jobs. Show everyone that you are willing to get dirty, too. When people see you doing the tough jobs, you will earn their respect.

6. Be Honest.

Truthfully explain why decisions are made. A lack of integrity and communication can lead to rumors, uncertainty, and distrust. Be fair and keep things professional versus personal.

7. Reward People.

All feedback must be given at the proper time. This is especially true for positive feedback or rewards. Some people require a simple *thank you*. Other people require more. Find ways to celebrate every accomplishment or visual display of growth. If you truly know (rule one) the people you lead, finding unique ways to reward them won't be a problem.

CHAPTER 32

COMMUNICATION IS THE KEY TO EVERYTHING

"Communication works for those who work at it."

– John Powell

My visit to Australia in 2006 was a life changing adventure. The memories are still burned into my thoughts. I talk about my adventures whenever the opportunity arises. One of my favorite experiences was my scuba diving adventure at the Great Barrier Reef.

Our ability to communicate in an understandable way is the determining factor to positive or negative experiences. Poor communication can lead to misunderstandings. Misunderstandings lead to communication breakdowns. Lack of communication limits growth.

I was in the resort town of Cairns, Australia. I had just completed my Rotary Group Study Exchange. I wanted to experience more of Australia, so I arranged to stay in the country for an extra week. Cairns is located near the Great Barrier Reef. It was something that I needed to see. My plan was to find a local charter boat to take me to the reef. I wanted to snorkel and take pictures.

I talked with the locals. They told me to go to the marina to investigate which charter company I should use. The tourist books all recommended the same charters. I went against their recommendations and selected a smaller charter company. When I approached their desk, the employees greeted me with huge smiles on their faces. I was treated as someone special from the first moment. They clearly explained to me how the tours worked. I was told to show up to the marina the next morning and be prepared to have a fun day.

When I arrived to the marina the next morning, I was ready to go. A fleet of charter boats filled up with hundreds of tourists. Many of the boats were over flowing. My boat had only twenty tourists. The boat was designed to hold one hundred people. The crew greeted us as we boarded. After a safety meeting, we were on our way.

It took two hours to get to the reef. The weather was perfect and the views of the ocean and mainland were spectacular. When we arrived, the crew asked who wanted to snorkel and who wanted to scuba dive. I planned to snorkel until one of the crew asked me, "Don't you want to scuba?" I responded, "I'm not certified." They told me that they could train me. This is when I remembered my grocery list:

~~Visit Australia~~

~~Visit the Great Barrier Reef~~

Go scuba diving

It was time for me to cross another item off of my grocery list. I was fitted for a wet suit. I was fitted for all of my scuba gear. I went through a brief class on how to scuba dive, how to use my equipment, dangers to avoid, and how to communicate underwater. Yes, communicate. We wouldn't be able to talk with our instructor underwater, so we were taught a series of hand gestures.

Some of the gestures were as follows:

Thumbs up meant that I wanted to return to the surface.

Thumbs down meant that I was ok to go deeper.

Putting my thumb and index finger together to make a circle and holding my other three fingers straight up meant that everything was ok.

If I wanted to go in a certain direction, I was supposed to point to my eyes first. Then I was supposed to point in the direction that I wanted to go. Next, I would wait for the ok sign from my instructor.

Putting my hands on top of each other and clasping my fingers together with my thumbs out wiggling meant that I saw a sea turtle.

Holding my hand in front of my face with my thumb touching my nose meant that I saw a clown fish.

Holding my hand against my forehead with my fingers sticking up like a fin meant that I saw a shark.

My first dive went well. I was underwater over thirty minutes. I was diving with an underwater camera that I purchased for my adventure. I took pictures of everything, including myself. When I was directed to return to the surface, I was a little sad. I wished that I had had more time.

As I got back on the boat, my guides asked about my adventure. I told them it was great. Then they asked me another question, "Do you want to do it again?" I took me a half a second to say yes. The boat went to a new location on the reef and I was back in the water again.

During the dive, I saw a giant sea turtle. I notified my instructor. I was given approval to swim near it and take a picture. I saw a giant clam and followed the same procedure. Then, I saw a clown fish. I alerted my instructor and I got a reaction that I didn't expect. Her eyes got large and huge amounts of bubbles came from her respirator. She shook her head no. I asked again and my instructor began looking around franticly. This is when I realized that I was giving the gesture for shark. We were in an area where sharks lived and the instructor's job was to keep us safe.

After recognizing my mistake, I waved my hands and made the proper gesture for clown fish. I pointed in the direction of the clown fish. My instructors face communicated relief. I took my picture and finished my dive. When we returned to the boat, we laughed about my miscommunication. My instructor said that it was easy to confuse the gestures when you get excited. She then gave me a great piece of advice, "think before you say something."

Communication isn't just verbal. People communicate verbally and non-verbally. People can write to communicate. Ideas and emotions can be communicated via voice tone and body language. Eye contact can display a variety of feelings. Communication is a skill people possess and use every day. Sadly, it is not something we work on everyday.

There are countless studies that say that *80% of all communication is non-verbal.* You will spend your entire life communicating with other people. This can be done face to face, via e-mail, by text message, over a telephone, or through hand gestures. Being an effective communicator greatly affects your ability to accomplish your dreams.

Communication is the process of successfully exchanging information, feelings, or ideas from a sender to a receiver. If one or both of the parties performs poorly during the process, misunderstandings will occur. The key is to perform the process effectively. I recommend that you always practice this important skill.

In this time of e-mails, mobile telephones, text messages, and social media, communication isn't getting better. In fact, it is getting more difficult to understand. If you really want to improve your communication skills, I recommend these three things.

1. Don't let technology be a crutch.

Humans are social creatures. Technology has facilitated and impeded our social abilities. It's easy to use technology, but technology doesn't allow a person to display emotion or other non-verbal forms of communication. At some point, you have to meet other people face-to-face. There will be no keyboard or keypad to assist you. Make the time to talk to friends and family in person. Create opportunities to be in the presence of other humans. The more you practice, the better you will become.

2. Take an Interpersonal Communication class.

When I was in college, *Public Speaking 101* was a requirement to graduate. Supposedly, I would learn to be a more effective communicator. That was false. The class teaches you how to speak in public. Speaking in public is the number one fear of people. Most people will never speak in front of a large group in their life.

When I started working at Lakeland Community College, I told all of the students to take *Interpersonal Communication 101.* I took the same class when I was a student. The class truly taught me how to communicate. My instructor, Barbra McEachern, was amazing. She told her students that we would communicate with others the rest of our life. She taught her students verbal and non-verbal communication.

The students were taught how to communicate one-on-one, in small groups, and in large groups. These are the activities that you'll be participating in your entire life.

3. Take an acting class.

I'm not recommending that you become an actor, but you can learn so much about communication by taking a class or two. In acting, you learn how to display and read emotions. You become competent in the art of communication. You interact with other people. You learn how to display thoughts and emotions verbally and non-verbally. Your practices can be recorded. It is amazing how you may believe you are displaying a certain emotion and your audience reads it differently. Acting is an art and skill, just like communication. The people who are effective are often rewarded.

To learn more about my trip to Australia and see some amazing pictures go to:

http://group6630.blogspot.com,

or

www.kitchenfrank.blogspot.com.

Click on **April 2006.**

CHAPTER 33

NOW HIRING... JUST NOT YOU!

"I can't imagine anything more worthwhile than doing what I most love. And they pay me for it."

– Edgar Winter

"Hi. My name is Frank C. Kitchen and my initials say it all. You should hire me because I am fun, creative, and knowledgeable. I create the environment that everyone desires to work in. If you need someone to plan your next event, train your staff, or motivate your employees, then contact me at hirefrankkitchen@yahoo.com. That's H-I- R-E Frank Kitchen, like the room, at Yahoo.com. No job is too big or too small. All I need is you and the opportunity to shine."

Those are the words I spoke on January 28, 2010. I was appearing on the cable news network *CNN*. I was a guest on *30 Second Pitch*. I had 30 seconds to tell the world on live television why I would be a great employee. After my appearance, I received e-mails from around the world. I received compliments. People thanked me for inspiring them. I also received offers for a variety of *pyramid schemes*. The one thing that I didn't receive was a legitimate job offer. I thought that the jobs offers would overwhelm me. I had nailed my live interview, but I was still looking for a job. That day made me realize that I am not defined by my job.

The jobs, careers, and work that you pursue have a huge impact on your dreams. In 2007, I left my job at Lakeland Community College to pursue my passion. I was going to be a full-time speaker. I saved my money. Contracts were lined up. I moved across the country to live with my future wife. Everything was going great until *The World Financial Crisis* hit. People were losing jobs, companies were filing for bankruptcy, and everyone was cutting their budgets. Not a good time to start a new business as a speaker.

My adventures as a professional job hunter began in 2008. My speaking calendar was very inconsistent. I was under-employed. I was working, but not enough to pay my bills. I figured that it would be easy for me to get a job to help make ends meet. I was armed with a great resume, a killer personality, a college degree, and a long list of accomplishments. I expected a great paying job with lots of responsibility.

I read countless articles about the changing job environment. The articles said that I shouldn't let my ego or pride get in the way of my job hunt. So, I applied for everything.

Here are a few of the jobs I applied for:

Painter, substitute teacher, toxic waste disposal, bank teller, event planner, product representative, solar sales, water sales, flight attendant, rental car sales associate, stadium tour guide, security officer, school crossing guard, street sweeper, personal trainer, audio and visual technician, hot air balloon employee, apartment rentals, youth mentor, human resources positions, speakers series director, zoo employee, sports league coordinator, secretary, office manager, youth mentor, personal assistant, pharmaceutical representative, acting coach, model coach, volunteer trainer, Student Activities Director, hotel manager, movie theater employee, waiter, public address announcer, pizza cook, valet, limo driver, delivery man, writer, golf course attendant, radio station representative, census worker, fundraiser, telemarketer, hospital baby photographer, birthday party host, and as a speaker.

I was turned down for every job above. No interviews, no decline letters, and no reason for why I wasn't good enough. I am a very confident individual, but my confidence was starting to wane. I was a National Keynote speaker, but was being turned down for *9-5 jobs*. I could train a company's employees at a conference one day. The next day, I would be turned down for a job as a corporate trainer. Why couldn't I get a job? Why couldn't I get an interview? Why couldn't I get a simple letter saying, "thanks, but no thanks"? I was no longer living the American Dream. I was living the American Nightmare. I was waking up to *The Employment Hustle*.

The Employment Hustle is what job hunters are experiencing everywhere. It's just like a board game. This board game has a major problem. There are numerous players, but only one player has the rules. That one player has the ability to change the rules anytime they want. That one player is known as *The Employer*. The only way for you win this game is to learn the tricks of the trade. You have to learn that your job is not your life.

You are not defined by your job. You are defined by your passions, pursuits, beliefs, and accomplishments. A job is a tool used to accomplish your dreams. When you start to think this way, you will be one step closer to living your dreams.

I applied for every job under the sun. It was the wrong thing to do. I wasn't getting any closer to my dreams. I was being desperate. Don't chase after the hot jobs listed on a website. Don't follow trends blindly. Don't listen to the people who say there is a *right way* to write a resume. You will find job fairs that don't have jobs. Job hunting is subjective. Employers have the upper hand because there are millions of people willing to work for anything. You have to pursue work that you are passionate about.

When you pursue a passion, it's not work. My best friend Scott is a golf coach. He loves to play golf. It's an expensive sport, but it's a passion. His father first taught him the game that he fell in love with. His dream is to play as much as possible and be the best that he can. To accomplish his dream, he started working at a golf course and coaching the local high school golf team. Both jobs allow him the opportunity to play all the golf he wants. It equates to thousands of dollars saved. He has truly worked to create a lifestyle. Scott is not simply working, he is living his dream. You have to work to create the lifestyle that you want. The best work opportunity for you isn't always posted on a jobsite. You have to go out and create it.

> *"The single greatest error and deception of our accounting system: people are paced in the liability column on the balance sheet. Machinery and computers are categorized as assets and people as liabilities."*
>
> — *The Dream Manager by Matthew Kelly*

You are not guaranteed a job. I thought that I was. I learned that an employer doesn't have to hire you. Personnel costs are the greatest expenditure for any business. Companies are cutting costs and trying to improve profits. They can layoff employees with a snap of their fingers. They can choose not to hire new staff when the costs are too expensive. You are seen as a liability. As a liability, you have to prove how you will help the employer build their dream or prove that you can make them money. For every job opening, there are several qualified candidates and hundreds of prospective candidates applying for the position that you want. A company is loyal to its stockholders and that is the bottom line. They don't have to give you a job. You can no longer expect to have a job. You have to earn it. During your job hunts, find employers to work with, not work *for*. When you work with someone, it's a partnership. You're working together to help build each other's dreams.

Scott created his opportunities. He befriended the right people and let them know about his passion for golf. Scott learned about his golfing jobs by networking. The United States Labor Department stated that 69% of job hunters acquired their jobs through networking or talking to someone that they know. Don't spend all of your valuable time searching job websites. The sites don't allow you to stand out from the crowd. Talk to the people that you know. These people know you well. They can give you a recommendation that a website can't. If 69% of employment comes from knowing someone, why do people spend the majority of their time seeking employment from people that they don't know? Focus your valuable time and energy on the people who care about you.

I want you to be armed with the knowledge needed to successfully survive the employment jungle. I want your dreams to become reality. Your lifestyle and career path will be a determining factor. You'll have to work hard, but it is more important for you to work smarter.

Nothing is guaranteed. The chances of you being with a company for life are slim. Don't base your life around your work. Pursue work where you will have more positive experiences than negative. Find an environment that you desire to work in. Take advantage of the job, and don't let it take advantage of you. Find work that allows you to use your special skills and talents. Find work that assists you with living your dreams. Pursue a passion. When you are passionate about something, it's not a job – you are hiring yourself to live your life.

CHAPTER 34

"THE TRICK OR TREAT THEORY"
THE 4RS TO A SWEET ORGANIZATION

❝Trick or Treat?" This is the question children ask countless homeowners nationwide on Halloween. Their question is answered when they receive a "fun-sized" treat. Many are ecstatic to receive a sugar filled confection that causes nightmares for dentists. Others say, "what is fun about this?" They've put in an enormous amount of time planning for Halloween. Children pick the best costume. They have to map out all of the good houses, they have to recruit friends and family to participate, and they have to obtain the perfect device to transport their haul of treats. All this work seems under appreciated when a 1 by 1 inch piece of candy is dropped into a king size pillowcase. The homeowner has failed to reward the children for the time and effort that they committed to impressing them. The child has been tricked: the *amazing* house on the corner did not deliver on the expectations it created.

A multitude of businesses are treating their employees just like the children mentioned. They forget that their success is based on time and effort of its employees. There is an old saying that says *"the business of business is people."* If a business truly wants to be successful, it needs to concentrate on the people that it employs. They must exceed their expectations. A satisfied group of employees leads to a successful business. To have the business of your dreams you must ask yourself this question: "am I a trick or a treat?"

"Putting too much emphasis on the bottom line is a mistake. Research indicates that good boss-employee relationships, opportunity and friends all rank higher than money on the list of what is important to employees in the workplace."

Tony Hsieh, CEO of Zappos

Here are four simple steps to increase the odds of creating the business of your dreams. I would like to introduce you to the 4 Rs.

1. Recruit.

You must attract the right people to support your cause or business. Just like Halloween, you must be creative in the way you attract people to you. Research what others are doing, and do something to make you stand out from the crowd.

2. Recognize.

Once you attract people to you, you must recognize what you have when you answer the door. Do you have pirates, clowns and super heroes? You may even notice the occasional teenager or parent! Every person you hire brings both known and unknown talents to the table. The key is to recognize the skills that they possess and how to use those skills to grow your business.

3. Retain.

When you move the letters around in the word *retain* you get the phrase *train e*. A big factor in retaining employees is proper training. When children arrive to your door for Halloween, you do two things: you organize them to receive candy one at a time, and you teach them how to ask the question, "Trick or Treat?" Constant training, organization, and clear communication will foster an environment where people feel valued and have an opportunity to advance.

4. Reward.

For employees, a paycheck is expected. When you do the unexpected, you create loyalty. People will spread the word about you. Be the house that gives out the unexpected for Halloween. This will create a buzz in the neighborhood. A full-size candy bar, a toy, crazy decorations, or an out of this world experience are the ultimate recruiting tool. There are many ways to reward your employees. The first three R's will help you learn if your employees are internally or externally motivated. Once you learn what motivates them, do the unexpected. If you want the more out of your employees, you must give more too. Make your business a treat to work for, and not a trick.

CHAPTER 35

LESSONS OF AN ACCIDENTAL MODEL

"Nothing is a waste of time if you use the experience wisely."
– Auguste Rodin

I was an "accidental model." I was *discovered* while spending a night out on the town with my friends. We were at a nightclub having a good time when several very tall and attractive women approached us. My friends magically disappeared. I felt as if I were being sacrificed. I discovered that the women were model scouts. They told me that I had a *good look* and should consider being a model. I immediately began looking for video cameras, because I knew a practical joke was being played on me. Fortunately for me, it was not a joke. I was given an invitation for an audition and the women left. As if by magic, my friends re-appeared to interrogate me. They had a hard time believing the offer, too. I put the invitation in my back pocket and I continued to enjoy the night with my friends.

The full story of how I got into modeling will have to be written in another book. The stories are funny, but the lessons I learned have been very important. Modeling taught me a lot about life and myself. One day, I'll be able to show my kids how Dad used to be cool. They will probably laugh and say "yeah, right!" That's when I will share the story of how I was an underwear model. On second thought, I will wait to tell them this story when they are thirty years old.

My adventure as an underwear model began when I was invited to model for a runway show. I was scheduled to model several outfits. Most were cool, and I wanted to keep some of the clothes that I was scheduled to wear. The charity event was being held to raise money for *Rainbow Babies and Children's Hospital.*

Every runway show required that the models attend a dress rehearsal. The rehearsals were held to practice routines and guarantee clothes fit properly. During the practice, one of my fellow models re-aggravated a back injury. Feel free to insert a joke here. The model was my friend Ryan. He was scheduled to participate in a routine where he would carry a female model. She would be in lingerie and he would be shirtless while wearing pants. After he was injured, I was told that I would be filling in for him.

I am not the biggest guy in the world, and being shirtless in front of a crowd made me very nervous and self-conscious. There were only so many push-ups that I could do at the last second to look bigger. Things got worse when I was told the routine was being changed. They decided to change the wardrobe. Part of me thought "yes!" Then, terror struck when I found out that I would be wearing very small boxer briefs! "Yes!" I would be showing off my push-up enhanced chest and my chicken legs. Did I mention the briefs had a lion on the front? The words *Roar* were written just above the lion. Very classy!

The show was going great when my number was called. The events were a blur. I remember hearing applause. I remember not dropping the half dressed model that sat on my shoulder. At the after party, several members of the audience came up to me. They made comments about me being the *underwear guy.* I thought the worst until I heard a sincere "you looked good!"

The experience was funny. It was also very educational. There will be moments in our lives when we will look back at an embarrassing moment and reflect. We will recognize how much we learned from that experience.

Here are a few lessons from my experience:

Lesson Number One: "Practice, Practice, Practice."

There is a science to walking the runway. It's not as easy as it looks. Every runway show that I have ever participated in had a rehearsal. It was the opportunity to practice. The more you practice, the better you get. I had to walk through my routines multiple times. I didn't want to fall off of the catwalk. I needed to practice good habits. The walk-through gave me the opportunity to learn and improve.

Lesson Number Two: "Embarrassing moments will happen."

You may not be caught in your underwear, but life is full of experiences you and others will find embarrassing. Take ownership of that experience. Live in the moment and use that moment to gain confidence.

Lesson Number Three: "Everything in life is a growth opportunity."

Even embarrassing moments can be used to gain strength and confidence. I can do almost anything in life now because hundreds of people saw me in my underwear. Nothing else in my life will be more embarrassing than that. Each time I fear something, I reflect back on that moment and the fear goes away and the laughter begins.

Lesson Number Four: "Don't run away from challenges."

I had the opportunity to turn down my "underwear moment." My dream was to be a successful model. Runway shoes and stepping out of my comfort zone are part of the job description. After the show, several opportunities opened up for me. I was invited to be in more shows. I made great contacts that led to more work. None of that would have happened if I ran away from the challenge. When we run away from our fears, we are really running away from our dreams. Challenges are put into our life to prove how badly we want something.

Lesson Number Five: "Always start with the right foot."

When walking on the runway, models are always taught to start with their right foot. You always want to take the right steps. Life is the same way: be sure to start the right way. People rarely get second chances or opportunities to do something. Make every moment count. Have confidence and look confident. Make a great first impression. Enjoy the moment and don't rush it. Take your time. I wanted to run down that runway as quickly as possible. Had I done that, I would have dropped the "lingerie angel" sitting on my shoulders. I had to stand up straight, be confident, walk slow, and start with the right foot. I was nervous, but I didn't give that impression to the crowd. It showed, because several of the models said: "I couldn't have done that, you looked so confident."

Lesson Number Six: "Celebrate."

After every show, there is a party. Parties are held to celebrate the night's accomplishments. Participants talk about what went right, share memorable moments, build relationships, talk about the future, and enjoy turning a vision into reality. My celebration was displayed by the smile on my face. I celebrated my personal growth. The shy kid from high school just walked a runway in his underwear and lived to tell the story.

CHAPTER 36

"SHARE THE VISION, LIVE THE DREAM"

"Where there is no vision, the people will perish."
— Proverbs 29:18

❝Share the vision, live the dream" is one of my favorite quotes. The man who said it wrote the forward to this book. His name is Rodger Campbell. He is one of the many people who inspired me to write this book. His quote inspires people worldwide to dream.

A dream is a cherished aspiration, ambition, or ideal. There are different names for dreams. People call them visions, goals, objectives, ideas, plans, targets, or fantasies. No matter the name, we all have them. Individuals and organizations are inspired by dreams. Many a dream has become reality. It takes just one person to get the ball rolling.

I have a former student and friend named Oloho. He felt strongly about the events of September 11, 2001. He was so moved by the events that he traveled to New York City shortly after the tragedy to see what he and a small group from his church could do. As the one-year anniversary of the event approached, he felt that our college should sponsor an event to honor the people who lost their lives on that day. He discovered that the college was having a small ceremony the morning of September 11, 2002. There would be a moment of silence; there would be brief words of remembrance, and the school flags would be lowered to half-mast. My student felt more should be done. He wanted the school to do more. His passionate convictions motivated him to action.

Oloho came to my office to talk about his dream for a Remembrance Program and a day full of activities. He wanted to know what he could do to make his dream possible. Oh, the questions he had. He described what he wanted to do in such detail that I could visualize everything in my mind. I was truly inspired. At that moment, we put together a list of everyone necessary to make his dream come true. We crafted a proposal to present to several departments and community organizations. Oloho displayed the same passion he had in my office to everyone he came in contact with. Before I knew it, he had organized a group of students and volunteers, reserved a venue, constructed a marketing plan, and recruited a Master of Ceremonies – me.

When September 11, 2002 arrived, the day began with the school holding its morning ceremony. After the ceremony, Oloho's events began. He made arrangements to have a memorial plaque and two twin evergreen trees dedicated on school property. He designed the plaque and picked out the stone that it was mounted to. It honored the lives of the people lost on that terrible day. The trees represented the beginning of life versus the end of it. During the day, he gave away tree saplings to anyone who wanted them. The theme of the day was to honor life, not to take it. The rest of the day consisted of Oloho and his volunteers informing classes and the community of that night's program.

Oloho was nervous when the program began, but he didn't need to be. The singers, dancers, and speakers performed to a packed house at the college's theater. He even recited a self-written poem that brought tears to the eyes of the people in the audience. When the night ended, people thanked the students for the day's activities. Many of the people discussed how professional and well-run the day's events were. They were amazed when they discovered the person responsible was a student. Oloho shared his vision and we all lived his dream. How exciting is that?

CHAPTER 37

LIFE IS A JIGSAW PUZZLE

〰〰〰〰〰〰〰〰

Have you ever had the pleasure or aggravation of putting together a jigsaw puzzle? They come in different sizes and forms. Some can be put together really fast and others take longer. Work and focus are required to put the pieces together. On the front of every puzzle box is a picture. It's the completed vision shared with you by the manufacturer. The box contains all the pieces to complete the puzzle. It's up to you to recognize how all of the pieces fit together to make the vision a reality.

Life is one complicated jigsaw puzzle. When you shop for a puzzle at a store, you search for a picture that appeals to you. You pick the vision that you would like to put together. Life is the same way. It will take time, but eventually you discover a vision you would like to see become reality.

The best way to assemble a puzzle is to work backwards. First, we need a vision or mission. Have you ever tried to assemble a puzzle when you didn't have the box? Just thinking about this makes me want to scream, but that's life. Remember the chapter on Mission Statements? If you don't have a vision of the completed puzzle, it becomes difficult to assemble the puzzle. Once you have a vision open the box, spread out all of the pieces and find a place to start working. Look at all the pieces to see what you have. At first glance, puzzle pieces can be confusing. The activity appears to be overwhelming, but as you're sorting through them, you start to notice how pieces fit together. Eventually, you start to piece together the vision.

Life is the sorting period for our vision. You have many pieces to sort through. This can be very frustrating. As you attempt to put pieces together, you experience successes and failures. You don't give up because you want to see the completed vision. You want your vision to become reality. Eventually, you have that "light bulb moment" where you *see* everything differently. The pieces start to go together easier. You recognize how they are supposed to fit together. Before you know it, the puzzle is complete.

To complete the puzzle of life, you have to focus on all of the relationships and experiences in your life. Take the time to notice how they fit together. Everything that happens to you in life can be used to learn and grow. This process can be frustrating, but life is a jigsaw puzzle. Once you recognize that everything that happens in your life is a piece of the puzzle, you must create a plan to sort the pieces and assemble them. There will be successes and failures, but like assembling a puzzle, some pieces fit while others don't. You must learn from your mistakes in order to avoid repeating them. You have to adjust and try again. Eventually, you will have that "light bulb moment." You will know what pieces you need to find. You will know how they fit together. You will start to assemble them and you will complete your puzzle. It will take time, perhaps a lifetime. There will be times when you may focus only on specific areas of the puzzle. But, in your mind, you will know that you're working to complete your grand vision.

CHAPTER 38

A PIECE OF MY PUZZLE

～～～～～～

As a child, I constantly dreamed about everything. I wanted to be an astronaut, a professional football player, a city planner, a businessman, an Olympian, a movie star, and someone who had a girlfriend. Some of my dreams were mere *flavors of the month.* Others have stayed with me throughout my life.

One of my dreams has always been to find *the One.* I wasn't looking for the character *Neo* from the movie *The Matrix.* I was dreaming of someone to spend my life with. You know what I'm talking about. I wanted someone to *share* my life with: a special someone who I could laugh with, a woman that I could explore the world with. That unique person who would love me for who I am and be there to put my teeth back in when I grow old.

I could be with anyone, but I was looking to spend my life with someone. I often wondered who that woman would be. I didn't sit around waiting for her to appear out of the blue. I had a life to live. I knew that I wasn't going to meet her sitting on my couch.

In the previous chapter, I stated how every person or experience in our life is a puzzle piece of our grand vision. My sister-in-law Kathleen is one of my puzzle pieces. She is the older sister of my wife Kelly. I met her in Las Vegas in 2004. I was in town celebrating my birthday with my friends. We were at the *Bellagio Hotel and Resort* celebrating and dancing the night away. During the festivities, I noticed Kathleen being harassed. I didn't know her at the time, but I did understand her body language. She and her friend Melissa were being hit on by a man who didn't understand the phrase "we're not interested." I approached and asked her if they needed help. They told the man: "we're with them." The ladies thanked us for helping them. They remarked about how our group looked like we were having fun. I told them how several of us were in town to celebrate our birthdays.

Kathleen and Melissa hung out with our group long enough to learn a few dance steps before they left. Being guys, my friends asked, "did you get their phone numbers?" You could see the disappointment on their faces when I answered with a "no." They razzed me, and we continued our night. I could have kicked myself for not getting their information. The little voice in my head told me that I should have asked for their phone numbers. About an hour later, the ladies returned. They informed us of how our group was fun and they would like to hang out with us some more. I was given a second chance. The night ended with an exchange of business cards and an invitation to hang out with the ladies the following day.

The next day, I called the number on the card. My friends and I were invited to a pool party at the *Monte Carlo* hotel. I asked my friends who wanted to go, but they all declined with a lot of stupid excuses. I decided to go… by myself. The pool party and day with the ladies was a good time. We spent some time by the pool having lunch and visited a couple of shops on the strip. My new friends asked me to keep in touch and I promised that I would. I thanked them for a good time and continued to vacation with my friends.

Six months later, I was in Las Vegas again with my best friend Scott. Melissa and Kathleen were in town, too. I had kept in touch with them through e-mail. We arranged to meet for lunch. Melissa was working at a convention, so we hung out with just Kathleen. This time we had lunch poolside at the *Mandalay Bay Hotel and Resort*. We talked about Las Vegas, how we met, my possible speaking career, and my dating life. I had just ended a relationship and was just looking to spend time with friends and family. Lunch ended and we thanked Kathleen for spending time with us.

When I returned from my vacation, I received e-mail from Kathleen. She thanked Scott and me for spending time with her while Melissa was busy. She also suggested that I meet her sister. She felt that we had a lot in common, and that we would hit it off. Never doubt a woman's intuition. Kathleen spent the next several months telling me everything about her sister Kelly. I was flattered by Kathleen's trust in me, but I lived over 2,000 miles away from her sister.

After months of friendly suggestions, I finally contacted Kelly. Kathleen had sent me her e-mail and phone number. We didn't hit it off instantly, but we had a good conversation. Over the next year, Kelly and I developed a friendship. The friendship developed into dating after I met her. Dating became a serious relationship. The serious relationship made me move across the country to live with Kelly. The next step was for me to drop down on one knee and propose to Kelly. A year after the proposal, we were married. During the reception, Kathleen talked about how we met during her toast. She talked about one of her dreams. The dream that Kelly and I would be together.

Make the most out of every opportunity and experience. You never know how it could affect your life. Life is a jigsaw puzzle. Every experience and relationship is a piece to that puzzle. You may not recognize how that piece fits the puzzle right away, but eventually, you will. Kathleen is a piece to my puzzle and I am a piece of hers. A random act of kindness can go a long way. That is why I have thanked Kathleen for her suggestion several times. I owe her a lifetime more.

Thank you Kathleen. My puzzle would be incomplete without you and your sister!

CHAPTER 39

ARE YOU LIVING YOUR DREAM?

"A dream that doesn't come true is a nightmare."

- Rodger Campbell

People are always looking for ways to motivate themselves. The first step to motivation is to look in the mirror. You must face yourself. Until you motivate yourself, no one else can motivate you. Other people can inspire you, but only you can motivate yourself to get started, to get out of bed, to believe in yourself.

The first action on the road to living your dream is taking responsibility. You cannot realize your dream until you make the decision to truly live it. We all have dreams, but dreams aren't reality until you take action and make them happen. It is okay to believe in a dream, but to be successful, you must take action and stay determined when you run into a roadblock.

In order to take action, you have to truly believe the dream you want to achieve. Many people are passionate about their dreams and really want them to become reality. When they don't see their dream materialize, they start to complain. This is the wrong action. Complaining is a waste of time. When it comes to your dreams, there are three actions to take:

1. Do Nothing.

2. Complain.

3. Do something.

Dreams put smiles on our faces, but as the old saying goes, "the only time *success* comes before *work* is in the dictionary." My wife and I go on nightly walks. Our quality time is highly valuable to me. I value my time with Kelly. I also value her comments and ideas. During our walks, we talk about anything and everything. We constantly talk about our dreams. One summer night, Kelly challenged me with the question: "are you living your dream?" This was in reference to me becoming a professional speaker. I dreamed of all the benefits of speaking, but I wasn't living my dream.

Living your dream, means you have to experience all of the ups and the downs before you can enjoy all the benefits. To enjoy the fruit of your labors, you have to put in all of the required work and effort. When you do this, you are truly living your dream.

Thank you Kelly for constantly challenging me to do my best.

CHAPTER 40

ARE YOU SPENDING TIME WITH THE RIGHT PEOPLE?

"You are the combined average of the people you hang out with the most."

– Jim Rohn

My mother always lectured me about hanging out with the right people. It's some of the best advice that a parent can give. We are a reflection of the people we spend the most time with. If you are around people who are chasing after and accomplishing their dreams, then you will achieve your dreams too. If you spend time around the right people, your dreams may happen faster than you thought possible.

I attended a diversity workshop in Cleveland, Ohio. The workshop coordinator wanted all of the attendees to meet each other. She had everyone participate in an ice breaker activity. The activity involved all of the attendees discussing where they were from and where they had lived. There was a state map of Ohio displayed on a wall. Our directions were to stick a colored piece of paper on the map showing where you had lived. I immediately asked for an entire pad of colored paper. Being the child of military parents made me a world traveler. The entire room was covered with neon green paper when I completed the icebreaker. The icebreaker led to conversations and the conversations led to new relationships.

Great relationships are developed over dinners, phone conversations, e-mails, and just hanging out. The military forced my family and me to constantly create new relationships. During my travels, I've cultivated great relationships. I've crossed paths with people who have impacted my life in positive ways. Several of these people are my friends.

In life, we come to know many people, but only a select few become our friends. I have many great memories with my friends. My closest friends have been there for me when I needed them. Over the years, they've become more than friends - they've become family.

As family, they are there to support me, and to point me in the right direction when I need a course correction. I am the person that I am today because of my family and friends. All of the time spent with them is very important to me. They have proven to me that life is about relationships and experiences.

When you put yourself in the right environment, you will grow. When you create relationships with the right people you will grow. If you are in the wrong environment, you are stunting your growth. Spending time with the wrong people will limit your opportunities to live your dreams. Remember what your parents told you: "be careful of who you hang out with."

Thank you to all of my family and friends. I hope that I've helped you and thank you for helping me.

CHAPTER 41

DID DRIVING SCARE YOU?

"Better to Face Danger than to Always be in Fear."
— Chinese Proverb

Courage is defined as the ability or strength possessed to do something that frightens us. People fear the unknown. They face situations that will frighten them daily: trying a new food item on the menu, moving away from family and friends, getting a gym membership, stepping out onto a dance floor, talking to a police officer, speaking in public, or asking questions. Fear can prevent people from having the opportunity to gain knowledge and new experiences.

Confidence in a person, situation, or dream comes from knowledge and experience. The youth of the world have many experiences where they display courage. There is a magical age when most teenagers display a lot of courage and don't recognize it. That age is 16. At 16, most teenagers are given the right to obtain a vehicle operator's license from their local Department of Motor Vehicles. This moment brings about frightful thoughts in the minds of parents worldwide. "Can we afford a car?" "How much will insurance be?" "Do we trust _____ with our car?" "What if _____ gets into an accident?" "There are a lot of dangerous drivers on the road!" "Have you seen _____ drive a go-kart?" These are just a few of the thoughts expressed or not expressed by parents.

While parents are freaking out, teenagers are imagining all of the possibilities. "I don't have to ride my bike." "My car will be just like the celebrities on MTV!" "I'm going to drive my friends everywhere!" "Mom and Dad don't have to take me to parties." "No more school bus!" "Road Trip!"

Children are fearless. This is the greatest time of growth. Children are often referred to as sponges. Children crave the knowledge necessary to make their dreams come true. They seem to ask millions of questions. If a child wants to know how something works, they will approach a stranger to ask questions: "why?" or "how?"

Parents actually teach their children to ask questions. Then, we start to grow up and fear the answers we may get. Many times, we don't ask questions because we fear the unknown. Instead of fearing the unknown, a leader embraces the possibilities of the future, just like the new driver. The new driver can fear all of the negatives of accepting the role of motor vehicle operator, or embrace all of the possibilities.

You will see many a teenager get into a "heated discussion" with their parents about how they will avoid all of the things that can go wrong. This is what a leader does. They don't fear all of the negatives and the unknown. They imagine all of the positives that can occur. At this point, they begin to grow. They gain new experiences that they would have never experienced if they had let fear hold them back. It is okay to acknowledge the fear, but also to think of all of the possibilities.

The next time you need a little courage to take action, reflect on your youth. You weren't perfect the first time that you drove a car. You were nervous, and a little fearful, of what could happen. Your parents' comments made you fear the unknown. Eventually, you began driving and, every day, you gained a little more confidence. The more you drove, the more courage you gained. Life and leadership are the same way. You look forward to all of the new experiences. Every new experience gets you closer to your dream. Every new experience increases your confidence and gives you the courage to pursue possibilities.

CHAPTER 42

DO YOU JOURNAL?

"Fill your paper with the breathings of your heart."
— *William Wordsworth*

My wife has given me wonderful gifts. One of the best gifts she ever gave me was a journal.

When I started writing this book, I began to look for ideas and inspiration. "What will I write about?" "Shouldn't it be called typing a book, not writing?" "How will I communicate my feelings?" I immediately went to my journal. My journal is the place where I write down all of my dreams and quotes that inspire me to accomplish my dreams. While going through my journal, I came across three entries:

"What do you believe in?"

"What are your dreams?"

"Go for it!"

Those quotes have been a few of the main themes of this book. They were a few of the puzzle pieces that I needed to put together to watch my vision turn into reality. For you to create your reality, you need a place to collect all of your ideas and thoughts.   Throughout this book, I've provided you with several places to write down some of your thoughts and dreams. Unfortunately, I didn't give you enough space. When you have time, I suggest that you go out and invest in a journal. Keep it close by. When that lightning bolt of inspiration hits, pull out your journal and write. Inspiration comes from hearing a song, reading a quote, seeing a picture, or even hearing a joke. The sad part is, just like lightning, it's gone as quickly as it came. To make that moment last for a lifetime, write about it in your journal.

You never know when you might need a good idea, need to remember a website, or just need that little extra push required to make your dreams come true. By writing down what is in your mind, you can go back and reflect. You can be inspired. You can be motivated. You can remember what you forgot. No matter how you do it, get the ideas out of your head and put them in a form that you can share with yourself and others. This includes a diary, journal, blog, notes, or doodles. It doesn't matter. Just get the ideas out. This is the first step to achieving your dreams.

Journaling is great. Many of the ideas in this book came from my journal. My wife gave it to me, because I told her about the millions of ideas in my head, and how hard it was to remember them all. I shared my vision, and now you are living the dream.

"Thank you Kelly, I love you!"

CHAPTER 43

"LIVE LIFE"

"Live life" is my motto. Nothing embraces this motto more than the quote below.

"Courage + Believe = Life." – John Challis

As I get to the end of this book, I am reminded of a quote I heard on *ESPN*. The cable sports network was doing segments on the 2008 Tampa Bay Rays and their journey to the World Series. Many of the players had written the quote "Courage + Believe = Life." It became the team motto. The quote was written under the brim of the team manager's hat. He got the quote from a Pennsylvania teenager. The teenager's name was John Challis.

John Challis was an average 16 year-old American high school kid. He loved sports. However, he also had a not-so-normal life. Doctors told him that he was going to die. He had a ten-pound cancerous tumor on his liver. That's bigger than a football. The cancer gave John a different perspective on life. During his senior year of high school, he joined the baseball team. When he was younger, he loved playing baseball. He stopped playing after being hit by pitches on several occasions. The fear of being hit by a pitch made him give up the game that he loved. His fears faded after a year and a half battle with cancer. Being hit by a ball was nothing compared to the life and death battle that he was having with cancer. Baseball was the sport he loved, and he wanted to play.

On April 11, 2008, John conquered his fear. At only 93 lbs, he was inserted into a high school baseball game as a pinch hitter. He wore a flak jacket to protect his tumor and ribs. He hit the first pitch that was thrown to him. It was a single between first and second base. While running to first base, he could be heard yelling, "I did it! I did it!" The RBI single would be the only hit of his baseball career. It was also his only at bat. His career stats were 1 for 1 with a batting average of 1.000 and 1 RBI. Under the brim of John's baseball cap, he wrote his motto: "Courage + Believe = Life" with his uniform number, 11. The motto would become the inspiration of people in the community and around the country. John didn't want people to feel sorry for him; he simply asked them to pray for him. He also wanted people to live life to the fullest. For John, fear prevented him from living. He learned that having courage and belief allowed him to truly live. John went on to receive his high school diploma. After a two-year battle with cancer, he passed away on Tuesday, August 19, 2008 at his home in Pennsylvania.

John Challis has inspired millions to accomplish one dream. He inspired people to live life to the fullest everyday. He was considered courageous because he didn't let fear prevent him from accomplishing his dreams. He recognized that he could only have courage once he believed. Even though his life was short, he went out and lived it to the fullest. This was only accomplished by his courage.

The more knowledge you have, the less fear you will have. Fear is the lack of knowledge or belief. Courage is gained when you can conquer a fear. For many, fear comes from the lack of knowledge or experience. Life is about experiences.

I truly hope this book gives you the courage to believe. Go out and live a life full of great experiences, and remember John Challis. Courage plus believe equals life.

For more information on John Challis, go to his website:

www.courageforlifefoundation.org.

CHAPTER 44

"STAY F.R.E.S.H."

"Fresh – slang for something that is exciting, appealing and great"

– Dictionary.com

Congratulations! You've come to the last chapter of the book. I hope the chapters in this book gave you fresh and creative knowledge on life and leadership. I hope they educated, inspired and entertained you to achieve your personal and professional dreams. Life is about leadership.

"Leadership is the ability to encourage, motivate and inspire an individual, group to build and develop a dream."

– Frank Kitchen

During your lifetime, you will be called on to lead. You will have to lead yourself and others. It will be important for you to stay *FRESH*. I want you to stay focused, resourceful, enthusiastic, strong and honest.

1. Focus

To achieve your dreams you need to avoid distractions. You must focus on what you need to do to turn your dreams into a reality.

2. Resourceful

To achieve your dreams you need to resourceful. You have to figure out the resources you have and the resources you need acquire. When you don't possess the skills, knowledge, finances or physical resources you need; get creative and find way to obtain what you need. Reach out to people you know and develop relationships with people you don't know.

3. Enthusiastic

To achieve your dreams you must be enthusiastic about them. You must show a passion, desire and commitment to turning the dream into a reality. You have to be positive. You have to think about what you can do, no what you can't do. You have to bring a positive, can do attitude. No enthusiasm, no reality.

4. Strong

To achieve your dreams you need be strong. Tough times are going to happen, you must stay mentally strong. Strength is something you build and develop. Are you connecting with people who are mentally strong or mentally weak? Where the mind goes the body will follow. You have to believe in what you're doing.

5. Honest

To achieve your dreams you need to honest. You need to be honest with the people around you, but more importantly, you need to be honest with yourself. You need to look in the mirror and admit that you can't do everything by yourself. You need to ask for assistance. You need admit when you're wrong. You need to admit your failures and areas you can improve. You need to admit why you are pursuing your dream. When you lie your dreams become a fantasy instead of a reality.

When you stay *FRESH,* you are living a life that is exciting, appealing and great. You are living a life where dreams flourish. I want to thank you for making the time to read this book and make one of my dreams flourish. I'd love to hear about the dreams you are pursuing and the dreams that you have achieved.

Frank

ABOUT THE AUTHOR

Frank Cornelius Kitchen has a passion for educating, inspiring and entertaining audiences about life and leadership. He has shared his fresh and creative knowledge with major corporations, colleges and universities, professional associations, conventions, conferences and leadership organizations in the United States, Australia and Canada.

Born in Bad Kreuznach, Germany, this military brat's constant travels led to very interesting life full of diverse experiences and relationships. Travel not only taught him how to connect with people, but also gave him visual examples of what it takes to "Live Life." He's been an actor, author, coach, educator, entertainer, entrepreneur, fundraiser, a master of ceremonies and professional model.

For almost 20 years, Frank has used his "Fun-Raising" style of teaching to help thousands individuals and organizations grow personally and professionally. A student leadership position in college quickly turned into a retail management and training career that evolved into position training and advising students and organizations at a small college in Ohio. His adventurous side led him to moonlight as an actor and model. Frank's love for education and entertainment forced him to make a huge decision. He left his college position to pursue a career as a professional speaker. His students and close friends to encourage him to pursue his speaking passion.

One of Frank's goals is to make the world a better place by sharing his knowledge and experiences. He uses his honesty, humor and creativity to make people laugh and learn at the same time.

A dedicated husband and father, Frank enjoys spending time with his family, traveling, reading, writing, teaching, and raising money for charities.

FUN FACTS ABOUT FRANK:

- Worked as a Birthday Party Entertainer in college
- Gave the commencement speech at his college graduation
- Award winning store manager for KB Toys
- Voted as one of "America's Most Eligible Bachelors" in Complete Woman Magazine and asked to audition for ABC's "The Bachelorette"
- Lead attempt to break the Guinness Book World Record for "Simon Says"
- Grew his hair out and had it dyed purple to raise money for Cancer Research
- Has appeared in ads for Nike, Goodyear, Toyota, Applebee's, Major League Baseball, The University of Phoenix, Waste Management and Phillips Medical
- Appeared on live CNN's "30 Second Pitch"
- Recognized as "Trendsetter" in Arizona Foothills Magazine

For information on Frank
(including booking him for your next event), please visit:

www.FrankKitchen.com

CPSIA information can be obtained
at www.ICGtesting.com
Printed in the USA
LVOW03s0606240118

563788LV00010B/187/P

9 781628 651676